Betania in My Heart

Betania in My Heart
Memories of a Mennonite School in the Mountains of Puerto Rico

Rafael Falcón, Tom Lehman
Editors

2023

Menohispana Collection

1. Puerto Rico: Island of Progress
2. La obra menonita en Puerto Rico, 1943–1981
3. Mennonite Memories of Puerto Rico
4. Memorias menonitas de Puerto Rico
5. Historia del menonitismo hispanohablante, 1917–1990
6. Growing up Mennonite in Puerto Rico: Nuestras Memorias
7. Hurricane María: Stories of Resilience and Compassion
8. They Made a Difference: Memories of Mennonite Workers in Puerto Rico
9. Betania in My Heart: Memories of a Mennonite School in the Mountains of Puerto Rico
10. Amo a mi escuela Betania: Memorias de una escuela menonita en las montañas de Puerto Rico

Titles in the *Menohispana Collection* are available at Amazon.com. Profits from the sales of these books are donated to Academia Menonita Betania.

CONTENTS

DEDICATION

To all the people who have made Betania a successful reality: administrators, teachers, staff, students, parents, and volunteers.

Rafael Falcón

Tom Lehman

And to Rafael, who passed away shortly before the completion of this book. Without him there would have been no *Menohispana Collection*.

Tom Lehman

Rafael Falcón, 1947–2022

ACKNOWLEDGEMENTS

We want to acknowledge Christine Yoder Falcón for her support and ideas for this project. Without her invaluable help this endeavor would have been impossible.

As always, we appreciate the contributions of our good friend and former Betania classmate Galen Greaser. His Mennonite and Puerto Rican connections, along with his willingness to help, make him a very special part of this book.

In addition, we would like to thank all the writers who gave their time and effort to share their memories with us, as well as those who contributed photos, information, and suggestions.

Special thanks to Nancy Myers and Galen Greaser, who proofread the book, correcting errors and suggesting improvements.

Finally an acknowledgement of Google Translate. When the call for contributions went out, authors were asked to submit their chapters in the language of their choice, English or Spanish. Just over half were in English, the rest in Spanish. Over the years Google Translate has improved to the point where the editors felt comfortable using it to produce rough drafts of translations in the other language, which went through the normal revision and editing process. This made it possible to publish separate English and Spanish versions of this book with the same content, something we could not have done if we had had to translate every chapter into the other language ourselves.

Rafael Falcón
Tom Lehman

PREFACE

Tom Lehman

This is a book of memories of Academia Menonita Betania, which many of us remember as Escuela Menonita Betania. Those privileged to attend or work there will recall their time at Betania as an important one for their early life and growth.

Many of the memories presented in this book center around several themes: the beauty of the location in the mountains of the Island, the food served in the cafeteria—with nostalgia for the crispy rice (*pegao*) and the universal dislike of the warm powdered milk—and the sports and recreational activities: the tetherball, softball, races, and swimming pool. Other memories center on the impact of the teachers, the crosscultural contacts between continentals and Island-born students, and memories of the school song "*Amo a mi escuela Betania*" (I love my school, Betania) and the "*Padre benigno*" sung every day before the noon meal. The lyrics for both songs are in an appendix, along with a link to online audio files of the music. Other memories are of the importance of the school in forming career choices, faith development, and lifelong friendships.

This book and its Spanish version are the final two books, volumes nine and ten, in the *Menohispana Collection* series. For nearly ten years, Rafael Falcón and I have been publishing books in that series that contain personal accounts of the Mennonite experience in Puerto Rico, where we both spent time growing up. We hoped that the series would help preserve memories of those who experienced and participated in that crosscultural project, which had an extraordinary impact on the Island and those who participated in it through the schools, hospitals, churches, and the *Luz y Verdad* broadcasts.

It is fitting that the last volume in the series is a book about Betania, where Rafael and I were students. Rafael was also connected to Betania as a teacher, the first Puerto Rican principal, and as a parent of two students who attended Betania. Betania has had a profound influence on many people. Over the years it has educated many who went on to contribute to the life of Puerto Rico, the professions, and the church, and some who have served around the world.

I would like to end with a personal tribute to Rafael Falcón, who passed away too soon, in August 2022. It was a privilege to work with him on this project. He was the one who had the idea of publishing a book of memories of the Mennonite experience in Puerto Rico. He knew whom to ask to contribute to the books. He kept coming up with ideas for additional books in the series. His humor, patience, planning, and organizational abilities made our collaboration on these books a pleasure. Those of us who knew him will miss him.

INTRODUCTION: THE EARLY HISTORY OF BETANIA

Rolando Santiago and Tom Lehman

The first Mennonites went to Puerto Rico in 1943 as part of the government's Civilian Public Service (CPS) program. They were conscientious objectors, seeking an alternative to serving in the military during World War II. They started the La Plata Hospital and worked in agricultural demonstration projects and community social programs. Although they were devout Christians, during the war they did not engage in evangelism, so as not to endanger their ability to serve in CPS.

When the war ended, the Mennonites planned a program of evangelism in Puerto Rico. After looking at a number of locations on the Island, Pulguillas was chosen as the place to begin the program. What is today called Academia Menonita Betania began as part of that mission program.

This introduction provides glimpses of the beginning and early growth of the school as reported by some of the early participants and observers of the project. In addition, Dr. Weldon Troyer, who as a young man witnessed the start of the effort, kindly shared his recollection of events in an interview.

Pulguillas Chosen as the Place to Start Mission Work

After 3 years [in the States] we were ready to return to India, but with World War II going on we were refused entrance permits. So we remained in Fisher, Illinois, at our practice, until the call came for us to spend a year under MCC in Puerto Rico. In December 1944, we landed in San Juan and were brought on our first trip to La Plata by Wilbur Nachtigall. During this first year Bro. S. C. Yoder visited P. R. and we made investigations for the need of mission work in this area. The Pulguillas community was chosen as a needy field to start with our mission work. Sometime before this, Don Antonio Emanuelli, ill with a heart ailment, came to La Plata Hospital for treatment. On leaving, much improved, he said, 'If ever I can be of service to you, let me know.'

(Dr. George Troyer in *Foundation Echo*, Mar. 1956, p. 13)

Don Antonio Emanuelli Donates Land for the Work

After a number of discussions on this location [Pulguillas], [and being unable to find land for sale], we finally decided to go to Don Antonio in August asking him for advice as to where we might obtain a small tract of land for opening work. After discussions and an explanation that we wanted it for a school, hospital, and church he said, 'If that is what you want it for, I will give you the land.' So arrangements were made to select a plot of ground the following week. When we returned to select the plot he said, 'I want you to pick the very best plot for your work anywhere on my land.' After investigation and listening to his advice as to what he thought to be the most suitable site, we selected a ten-acre plot just across a deep ravine from the coffee hacienda.

(Dr. George Troyer in "Report from Puerto Rico," from the *Report of the Fortieth Annual Meeting Mennonite Board of Missions and Charities*, 1946, p. 16)

Building Begins on the Property

The property had trees, some coffee plants, and bananas growing near the road; there was an open grazing area further up from the road. A bulldozer was brought in to scrape away the grass to make a drive from the road up to the flatter property above. Fred Springer, Dr. George Troyer, Elmer Springer, some other people, and I flattened it out and smoothed it. Later on gravel or stone was added. Originally the drive was perpendicular to the road. When the pickup went up, you had to get a running start. Later the drive was moved further east to make the more slanted drive that exists today. For the first couple years there wasn't electricity or running water. Water was brought in by pickup in 60-gallon barrels.

To save money the concrete blocks were made on site. There was a cement mixer, and José (Josian) Delgado mixed the cement, gravel, and water and put the concrete into a block maker that made the blocks. He made thousands and thousands of blocks that were used to make the buildings.

(Dr. Weldon Troyer interview, February 28, 2023)

———

The first building was a concrete home built by Joe Brunk for Paul and Lois Lauver who arrived in Puerto Rico in December of 1946. He built two other concrete buildings, one for the Springers. Brunk also built a frame cottage for others to live in. In 1946 two garages were built and a Sunday School was started in one.

Later that year an open-sided tabernacle was built. It was dedicated on August 25, 1946, with S.C. Yoder, President of the Mennonite Board of Missions and Charities, in charge of the service.

By the summer of 1947 the building program on the property was complete. There were three large concrete residences, two frame cottages, the tabernacle/church building, a two-room clinic and a milk station building.

(Justus Holsinger, *Serving Rural Puerto Rico*, p. 210)

Betania School Opens

During the summer of 1948, Beulah Litwiller, a newly-assigned missionary, began preparation for the opening of a mission school at Pulguillas. The tabernacle-church building was walled in, and tables, benches, blackboards, and teachers' desks were made by the local carpenters. The Pulguillas Christian Day School was opened August 16, 1948, with an attendance of twenty-eight pupils, eighteen in the first grade and ten in the second. Several weeks previous to the opening of the school, the teachers, Beulah Litwiller and Mrs. Elmer [Clara] Springer, went from home to home selecting those children who they felt would be an asset to the school. Most of the children selected were already attending Sunday school and were children of parents in sympathy with the church program. Each child was required to pay a tuition fee of three dollars a year. This fee did not cover the costs of instruction but it helped the parents to value and appreciate the school facilities.

In addition to meeting the three hours of recitation required by the Department of Education, the school offered a half hour of religious education each day. The religious instruction included Bible stories and choruses. An inspector from the Department of Education visited the school in January 1949. He was well pleased with the work and recommended recognition of the school by the Department of Education.

(Justus Holsinger, *Serving Rural Puerto Rico*, pp. 211–212)

In the first year, the day began at 8:30 a.m. with an opening devotional period when all students gathered. After the opening period, the children went to their separate classrooms, where they had Bible study. The remaining subjects were taught from 9:00 a.m. to 12:00 p.m., with the last twenty minutes spent singing or doing handwork. At 10:15 a.m., the students had recess, and at 10:25 a.m., they had a snack and a rest period.

(Gladys Widmer, "A Report of Mennonite Board of Missions Activities in Puerto Rico." Mennonite Board of Missions, 1951)

The School Grows

The plan has been to add a grade each year to the school. Accordingly, the third grade was added in 1949, the fourth grade in 1950, and the fifth grade is to be added in this coming school year of 1951. The first two grades have met in the mornings with the third and fourth grades meeting in the afternoon. Additional teachers were added as needed each year.

With the completion of the new church building in September 1949, the old building was used exclusively for the school. Forty-four children were enrolled during the second school year and fifty-six during the third.

(Justus Holsinger, *Serving Rural Puerto Rico*, pp. 211–212)

———

In 1950, Anna Kay Massanari arrived to serve as a teacher for the third year of the school's existence. Beulah Litwiller went on furlough in February of 1951, and Carol Glick arrived in August of the same year to serve as school principal for its fourth year. This year, the school constructed a new building.

(Gladys Widmer, "A Report of Mennonite Board of Missions Activities in Puerto Rico." Mennonite Board of Missions, 1951)

———

November 5, 1951, marks the moving day into the new, hurricane-proof building. As I stand on the lawn of the new three-room school, children large and small come trooping out the door of the old building with an article to be moved to the new school. Here come several carrying tables. Others are carrying benches upside down on their heads. There go several racing down the hill for another load.... It is 11:00 and nearly everything is moved. After singing and dedicating our new building in prayer to the glory of God and the building of His kingdom, the children will go home with a sense of having moved 'their' school.

Tomorrow seventy children in five grades will come here to study, work, sing, play, and pray.

(Carol Glick in Gladys Widmer, "A Report of Mennonite Board of Missions Activities in Puerto Rico." Mennonite Board of Missions, 1951)

————

When the bell rings, we gather in our rooms for a 15-minute devotional period before the regular classes begin. In grades one through six the day is spent in the usual grade school classes. In seventh and eighth grades, Home Economics and Industrial Arts are added to the curriculum.

The school has an enrollment this year of 165 students and has 8 grades. In all Puerto Rican grade schools the children go only one half day; one group in the morning and one in the afternoon. This is done so that more children will get to go to school. In the Pulguillas school, however, all but the first and second grades go all day. All the children eat in the school dining room at noon. The food is supplied by the government, like in the public schools.

Besides those who come from the Pulguillas community, children come from 8 other communities. The school has two small trucks which have been equipped for hauling children. These trucks bring children from the five most distant communities. Although some of the children come from some distance, most of the children walk to school since they are from the Pulguillas and surrounding communities.

(Fred Springer in *Foundation Echo*, Jan. 1955, p. 11)

———

Eight years ago a first and a second grade had their first classes in Bethany Mennonite School. In April the youngsters who were then second graders graduated from ninth grade to go into the public schools for their senior high school education. Seven out of 12 are continuing this year in the public schools.

Since that first year another grade has been added each year. This required, according to the standards of Puerto Rico's Department of Education, the addition of new staff members as well as additional rooms. For the year 1956–57 five teachers are being used for grades one through six. Fifth and sixth grades are still in one room. The junior high school's departmentalized program requires five teachers, including the principal.

The school is housed in three one-story buildings built on three different levels on the mountain. The first building is for first and second graders; the second, for third to sixth grades; the third, overlooking the others, contains space for grades 7 through 9, as well as home economics laboratory, library, and office. A small shop and the dining room complete the campus buildings.

This year a new continental teacher is being added to give the 28 children of continental parents instruction in English reading, language, and spelling since the daily English classes are not suitable for children whose mother tongue is English.

(Carol Glick in *Foundation Echo*, Nov. 1956, p. 3)

Although this book is centered around memories of Betania, the editors hoped that it could help document the history of the school. The final chapter, by Antonio Zayas Bermúdez, Ed.D., the current director of Betania, records the recent trajectory of the school. Two appendices, one a list of the school directors and another of ninth-grade Betania graduates, are additional attempts in that direction. It was not possible to obtain a definitive list of all Betania graduates. The list presented was compiled from school yearbooks available to us, as well as two classes whose members were able to provide the names of some of the graduates. We apologize to the graduates not included. We felt that giving the names of some of the graduates was better than not listing any. A final appendix contains a selection of early Betania photos, the buildings, teachers, students, and school activities. In addition to the photos included in the book, there is an album in Tom Lehman's Flickr collection called "*Academia Menonita Betania*" with over 600 photos, most in color, having to do with the school, its people, buildings, and grounds. It can be seen at https://bit.ly/3YnR1d4.

Original version in English

1

BETANIA'S IMPACT ON ME

Mark Nissley

I arrived at Betania in 1963. Our family had left La Plata in 1961 after five years there and gone to Goshen so Dad could get a couple of years of seminary training to help with his pastoral role. While we were in Goshen I went to first and second grade at Parkside Elementary, by the South Side Soda Shop.

We came back to Puerto Rico in 1963. I was excited to go to Betania because I looked forward to reconnecting with my childhood friends from La Plata. These would have included Johnny Snyder, Becky and Betsy Rivera, Johnny Driver, Rolando and Ricardo Santiago, Steve Nafziger, Harvey Hernández (Doña Esperanza's son), and the Beachy boys. These kids had been my buddies in La Plata for five years. When we got to Betania in the fall of 1963, my brother Tim was in first grade, Ruth was in second, and I was in third. It turned out that not one of my childhood buddies was in my class. All these people were either a year older or a year or so younger. What? That was so unexpected. I had never considered this possibility.

When we returned to Puerto Rico, we stayed the first few weeks in the Heisers' residence, the pastor's house at Pulguillas. Next, we lived in La Cuchilla for several months. This house was on the road to Palo Hincado, along the sharp, steep ridge for which the La Cuchilla area was named. The house was at the top of the ridge, and clouds would come right through the living room. A building next door had been Dr. George Troyer's clinic. The neighbors who lived in the former clinic were José María and Iraida Ortiz. I believe they were newlyweds at the time. We got to know these great people as neighbors early on.

The bus that went from Betania to La Cuchilla was a Volkswagen microbus. Like the VW Beetle, the motor was in the back. A platform over the top of the engine provided some storage area. Since the bus seating was fully assigned by the time we moved to La Cuchilla, we Nissley kids got the "special" seating on the shelf over the motor, where we had to recline to fit in. We rode that way for part of the year, back and forth from La Cuchilla to Betania. Mr. Israel Hernández was the bus driver. He was a teacher at Betania and, I think, also a pastor at Palo Hincado. His daughter Gladys and son Héctor were in my class at the school.

My first impressions of Betania were unbelievable! I couldn't believe that one side of the classroom had folding walls that opened from floor to ceiling. On nice days they would be completely open. The view was to the hillside across the creek, where the Bonillas now have their farm. It was a steep hillside with cattle and cow paths, just an incredibly pastoral setting. I couldn't believe how cool it was, so different from Parkside School in Goshen.

My teacher for the first year was Mr. Fernando Luis Cains. He didn't tolerate any breach of discipline. He had a saying that my classmates remember to this day. He could be writing on the blackboard, and if he heard someone whispering in class, he would whirl around and crisply say, *"Se me quiere callar"* ("Would you please be quiet.") It was generally quite effective in getting the person to hush up. Many of us remember that and can still imitate the way he would say it.

A memorable story about Mr. Cains involves the bus commute from Betania to Coamo, where he lived. The student bus from Coamo to Pulguillas was one of the modified covered *camiones* (trucks). The trucks had welded pipe steps in the back that were raised and lowered so riders could get on and off. We soon learned it was important to keep your fingers out of the way when the steps were raised and lowered. Two rows of wooden benches, running from front to back, faced each other. Mr. Cains sat near the ladder, supervising who got on and off the bus. He was the definitive authority and maintained well-ordered discipline as we rode and as people got on and off. He was no small figure to be reckoned with. He had a lot of presence, a lot of gravitas. He was as black as could be, with hair as white as could be, with a dignified and often serious countenance. He could laugh and have fun, too, but if you were not in his good graces, he could be quite stern.

On the Coamo route, fellow passengers included María and Enid González, Raúl Santiago, a guy named Valentín, the Feliciano boys, and the five Ortiz kids—they were Domingo and Margo's kids, also nephews to Enrique Ortiz. They were Tato, Chiqui, Elí, Edgardo, and the youngest, Aidita. There were other kids, and I don't remember all of them, but the bus was packed.

Dave Bauman was the driver in 1963, our first year. The *camión* would wind down Route 14 from Asomante to Coamo, with nothing but downhill and switchbacks until you got to Las Calabazas. The Ríos house, where the Ríos girls and Ricardo Cabrera lived, was there, and the Felicianos lived just further on. That is where the road leveled out and you crossed the Coamo River, and then you were in the flats (*los llanos*) the rest of the way to Coamo. So when we crossed the bridge over the Coamo River, we'd pound on the back of the truck so the driver could hear us and we'd all say "*Ahora Bauman*" ("Now Bauman"). This was our call for him to give it the gas.

One time it was pouring sheets of rain when we got down to *los llanos*. We had a flat tire and had to pull over and stop. Some of us boys wanted to get out and watch Dave change the flat tire in the rain. Mr. Cains informed us that nobody was getting off the truck. Everybody was going to stay put. We weren't going to get past Mr. Cains because he had laid down the law. The enclosed seating area of the bus had two windows on each side made of plywood in wooden tracks, not glass or screens. Normally the windows were open, but not when it was raining. Boys being boys, some of the Ortiz boys and I thought we might be able to get out through the side window. The side window in front seemed best since it was farthest from Mr. Cains. So, out the window we went.

That worked pretty well. We ran around in the pouring rain, got soaked, and watched Dave Bauman changing the tire. Great fun! When the tire was fixed, Dave got back in the cab, and we needed to get into the back of the *camión*, but Mr. Cains was there. Getting past Mr. Cains wasn't going to be easy. There was no way to get in without getting him wet. We were soaked. We got him wet. He was not thrilled.

The next day at school, word came to our classrooms that we were to report to the office. And so Edgardo and I, Elí, Tato, and Chiqui met at the principal's office. The situation was discussed, and paddling was determined to be the appropriate consequence for our lack of discipline and obedience. I had not yet been paddled at Betania. This was my first time. They explained it to us. Mr. Gerald Wilson could choose from various paddles hanging on the wall. He selected one, and then we walked with him to the recreation building, where there was enough room for us to stand in a row with our hands on our knees. We formed a row lined up

4

by age, Tato, then Chiqui, then Elí, then me, and then Edgardo. We didn't want to cry or lose face in front of the others.

The paddles were maybe six inches wide and over a foot long. At the bottom, they had a handle like a baseball bat. Another feature of the paddles was that they all had round holes in them, an inch or so in diameter. I don't know if that was to make the paddles lighter, to let them go through the air faster, or to make them sting more. In any case, when you got home after an encounter, you could drop your pants and see these circles imprinted on your bottom.

Mr. Wilson started with Tato. Tato was determined not to cry, so he got another lick. Mr. Wilson continued until Tato began to cry, after maybe six or eight licks with the paddle. Chiqui was next. He had noticed that the paddling continued until Tato began crying, so on the very first lick with the paddle, Chiqui started crying. Mr. Wilson stopped and went on down the row. We all imitated Chiqui and started crying as soon as the paddling began.

When the paddling was done, Mr. Wilson told us we could take time to reflect on the reasons for this discipline. As soon as he left, Chiqui, always the clown, started doing a little dance and saying, "*Eso a mí no me dolió na'.*" ("That didn't hurt me a bit.") At that moment, Mr. Wilson opened the door to look in on us because we didn't sound like very sad boys. He said perhaps we needed a few more licks. Right away, Chiqui went straight from laughing to crying. The rest of us were giggling, covering our mouths with our hands, trying not to let Mr. Wilson see us. We were all shaking with laughter at Chiqui's quick changes. If Mr. Wilson did see us, he must have decided to have mercy. He closed the door and went back to his office.

So that was my introduction to this form of discipline at Betania. I suspect that after that experience, it didn't seem threatening enough to keep me from falling into more mischievous escapades, which led to me encountering more of that discipline. I received the benefits of paddling numerous other times during the following years.

The third, fourth, and fifth grades were in the long building below the softball field. Below that was the building where my brother Tim and sister Ruth attended first and second grades that year. The following year, 1964, my class moved into the middle room for fourth grade. Mr. Héctor Vargas was the fourth-grade teacher. He was friendly and maintained good discipline. Sometimes he displayed some impatience with us, no doubt due to our "perfect" behavior during class. That was the year Federico Rosado came and joined our class. I have Betania yearbooks for every year from fourth grade on, and I still enjoy looking at pictures of those days and have wonderful memories of our classmates.

Recess was always a great break from sitting still. The swing set at Betania was quite tall, with long chains coming down to the seats, so you could get some real height when swinging. Those were the most fun swing sets I was ever on. Other swing sets paled in comparison. Ours were awesome! Next to them were the teeter-totters, which had three notches in the center, so if you had a bigger person on one side, you could set it off a notch to equal out the weights and balance more easily. However, both of those were pretty tame compared to *bola de puño* (tetherball). That really got your heart rate up.

I was not an outstanding athlete in traditional sports like softball or basketball. In fact, I tended to be among the last picked for any of the teams. But *bola de puño*, now that was another story! I was good, motivated, and fiercely competitive. In fourth and fifth grades, at recess, there was usually a line for the *bola de puño* courts. There were two of them. Each court had a round concrete pad with a line down the middle. You had to stay on your side and try to wrap the ball around the pole and keep the other guy from doing the same. If you won, you played against the next person in line. I always wanted to win so I could keep on playing. It was hard to win against a couple of the taller guys like Bobby Álvarez and Guillermo Santiago. Guillermo was left-handed and tall, and it threw the game off to be playing against a left-hander. *Bola de puño* was my sports passion during fourth and fifth grades.

One time my fifth-grade teacher, Mr. Heriberto Santiago, a wonderful teacher, determined that I was being a little too competitive and that my behavior was unsportsmanlike. He grabbed me by the ear and walked me down to the fifth-grade room. He led me to my seat and, in clear language, counseled me to consider the relative importance of the game and my poor behavior playing it. Being dragged by the ear was another unforgettable form of discipline. It was painful and humiliating to be taken away like that in front of everyone. Truth be told, I probably liked that less than paddling.

Mr. Santiago taught that grade for many years, maybe for decades. Everyone who had him as a teacher spoke highly and warmly of him. He was the first one who told me, *"Tú debes ser abogado."* ("You should be a lawyer."). He noticed I had quick explanations to defend and justify myself whenever I was being chastised. He recognized that ability and told me that. I have very fond memories of him.

After Mr. Wilson, our next principal was Mr. Merle Sommers. The Sommers family had been next-door neighbors when we lived in La Plata. They came to Betania when I was in fourth or fifth grade, and their oldest daughter Lynn was in my class, so I finally had a childhood friend from my time in La Plata in our class at Betania.

I'll never forget the time Mr. Sommers used a clever and effective technique in determining a course of discipline. Mark

Baer and I had been sent to the office for something we had done. But this time, Mr. Sommers talked with us in a reflective tone and asked, "What would be the best discipline for this? What do you boys think would be the best discipline?" Mark and I looked at each other and said, "Um, you could make us feed the hogs." Mr. Sommers wasn't sure about that. "What else might be a good punishment? Are there other punishments you could think of?" "Um, you could make us sweep the sidewalks." Well, we suggested every possible thing other than paddling. None of them seemed quite right. He just wasn't sure. "Was there anything else?" And finally, we reluctantly said, "You could paddle us." That one seemed like the best one, so we got a paddling. He got us to tell him what punishment we liked the least by asking our counsel about a suitable punishment.

Somewhere around fifth or sixth grade, the years of the *camión* ended. We now had a four-row van, like today's church vans. The driver by then was Dave Hartzler. The van would be parked in front of our house overnight, and Dave would come down from the Voluntary Service house (Dr. Troyer's former place in Aibonito) on a Vespa scooter in the morning and drive the Coamo students to school in the van. Then he'd take us back to Coamo after school.

Depending on your behavior, you could sit where you wanted. If you had not been on good behavior, you sat in front with Dave. One time, my sister Ruth and Stephanie (Fanny) Rivera were sitting in front with the driver. Whatever behavior had caused them to be sitting up there was continuing. They were doing different things back and forth until Dave said, "Will you stop that." My sister said, "She pinched me." Dave said, "Did you pinch her, Fanny?" Then he laughed and said, "Maybe I should ask, 'Did you pinch her fanny?'" That was in English, but we all got the double meaning and laughed.

After fifth grade, the next class was sixth, in the green building up past the principal's house. That building housed the sixth and seventh-grade classrooms, with the sixth at the front end. The back was the seventh grade and the biology and science room, where Royal Snyder taught. Going up to the sixth-grade building was leaving behind what had been familiar for my three years at Betania and moving to what seemed a higher level.

Mr. Ángel Alvarado was our sixth-grade teacher. He had not been teaching very long. I remember that our classroom had *un espacio* (a space) at the top of the side walls, where the roof met the walls. One time during class, students started looking and pointing upward. A snake had gotten into our room near that area. That was a major distraction, and I remember Mr. Alvarado trying to keep discipline with the snake there. It was not working very well, and I believe he let us out early for *recreo* (recess) while the snake was chased off.

I encountered him many years later at the Aibonito Mennonite Church when I was in Puerto Rico for a visit. An older man came up to me and said, "*¿Marcos Nissley, se recuerda de mí, quien soy?*" ("Mark Nissley, do you remember me, who I am?") It was Mr. Alvarado. After he told me, I recognized him, and we enjoyed reminiscing about our Betania days.

Our seventh grade was in the next room at the back end of that building. I forget whether Miss María H. Rosado or Mr. Snyder was our homeroom teacher, but by that grade, different teachers taught different subjects, so it wasn't just one who taught all the courses for the class.

During that year, I developed a lifetime friendship with Edwin Deliz. We both played guitar and became the regular guitar players for chapel down at the Pulguillas church. We sat in front to accompany the *coritos*, often led by Alicia Kehl. Edwin had a quick sense of humor, as did I.

In seventh grade, we started a game that continued through our remaining years there. The game was, you were "it" until you could get the other one to laugh. Once they laughed, they were "it" until they could get you to laugh. We got better and better at keeping a straight face, even when the other one was doing hilarious things. This meant that as time passed you had to do more outlandish things to get the other one to laugh. And so, over the years, we accrued quite a bag of tricks, including inventing nicknames for every teacher.

I still remember most of the nicknames. We would say something like "Mr. (nickname), can I go to …" and say the nickname quietly so only Edwin or I could hear it, not loud enough that the teacher could hear it. Eventually, one of us would do something funny enough that the other guy couldn't help but laugh. If the teacher was writing on the blackboard, one of us might get up and do a jumping jack and sit back down quickly, hopefully before the teacher caught us. Sometimes the teacher would turn around as we were sitting down, and we'd have to act like we were just stretching or something. That was our fallback game if we were bored. It entertained us and some of our classmates who observed our antics.

During the last few years, there weren't enough students coming up from Coamo, so they discontinued the school bus service from there, and we had to use the *guagua de Jaime*, the public bus. It was so slow it couldn't get out of its own way. We had to take an early bus to Asomante. When the Aibonito school bus came, it would pick us up there and take us to Betania. That was not nearly as much fun as when we had our own bus.

One of those last years, when Miss Glick was principal, I was sent up to the office from the seventh- or eighth-grade classroom, as my behavior was such that I needed to be sent out of the room. I think Miss Rosado sent me up so she could go on teaching her class. When I got to Miss Glick's office, she took an unusual tack, which made me nervous. She leaned back in her chair and said, "Well, Mark, how are things with your family?" I answered, "All right, I guess." "Well, how's your dad liking his work, and how are things with your dad at home?" I was really confused and puzzled. I didn't know where this was going, and I was concerned because she was asking about my family and my dad. "And how is your mother doing? How is she enjoying living in Coamo?" I just was not sure why she was asking these questions. It didn't seem like a good sign. And she asked about my brother and sister—how did they like Coamo and Betania. I responded briefly to each question, getting more and more worried about the direction this was going. It didn't seem like a normal disciplinary conversation. Finally, she said, "Mark, you know, you're really not bad, you're just mischievous. You're restless and can hardly help yourself sometimes. Go ahead and go back to class and just try a little harder." I was so surprised.

Years later in my life, I would remember that statement. When I was in trouble with authority and was questioning my character and future, I remembered her words, that I wasn't really bad; I was just mischievous. Those were affirming words at some critical times. When I needed them, those words were there for me to remember.

In ninth grade, we had Mr. Rafael Falcón as our homeroom teacher. His youth and good-natured ways with us made it sometimes seem like he was more than a teacher; he was also part of our class as a good friend.

By the time I got to ninth grade, a number of us had been together for a long time. There was Bobby Miller, Bobby Álvarez, Federico Rosado, Ellen Graber, Edwin Deliz, Olguita Jiménez, Dennis Heiser, Haydeé Suárez, Linda Thompson, Leonardo Chiesa…. We had become a pretty tight group of friends. After lunch at the *comedor* (dining hall), we would often gather under the *flamboyán* tree and sing songs we knew. Edwin and I would pull out our guitars, and we'd all join in singing "*En Mi Viejo San Juan,*" The Rolling Stones tune "As Tears Go By," and other songs we knew.

We were very aware that this was our last year at Betania. It felt like the end of an era; an important part of our lives was drawing to a close. Our time felt precious and priceless almost every day. We knew that our days as a group together were numbered. We would be going off to different places. We weren't happy about that. We were nostalgic and missing each other even before we were gone, loving the time we could still spend together. We had crushes on the girls; we had good friendships with the guys, and we'd gone through all these years together. So those were special and memorable times.

Over the years since then, our class has continued to get together, maybe more than any other Betania class. It was not a tradition at Betania to have alumni events, but the first time I returned to Puerto Rico, years later, I visited some of my classmates and said, "Let's call our other classmates; I want to see the others too." So we called everybody we could and had a reunion. I think the first one was at Olguita's house, and the next time I was down, we had one at Bobby Álvarez's place. I remember someone said it was great when I visited because it gave an excuse to call everyone and get together.

And we had a great time when we got together. We remembered all the escapades with the teachers, doing class activities and class trips, telling stories of who got in trouble for what and what punishments they got. It just continued to increase our bond, and we continued to have reunions, not annually, but every so often. Whenever I was planning a trip, I'd call ahead and let them know I was coming, and we'd make some arrangements.

By then, the classmates had spouses and kids. So later on, our reunions were on a bit larger scale. We'd rent a beach house for a weekend or a whole section of a beachside motel. The last one we had was at La Parguera, on the southern coast of the Island.

I have so many memories of Betania, most of them good. I was shaped and profoundly impacted by my time there. We were blessed with Christian teachers who cared for the students and worked with an administration committed to showing God's love. We were challenged by the high academic standards and stimulated by the wonderful outdoor campus in the central mountains of Puerto Rico. I am so grateful to have been part of this Betania community. I will never forget those days and the many people we interacted with. They are, even now, still precious to me.

Original version in English

2

MEMORIES OF MY STUDENT YEARS IN BETANIA

Dr. Fernando Juan Echegaray Daleccio

The Betania Mennonite Academy excels as a school because of the diversity of approaches it uses in teaching. The integration of academics, sports, and the teaching of Christian love has been the perfect combination for its success. These essential values have been the key to the comprehensive development of good men and women who serve society today.

In 1971, I began studying in the second semester of fifth grade at the Betania Mennonite Academy. I was ten years old at the time. The school principal was Ms. Carol Glick, and Mr. Heriberto Santiago (RIP) was our homeroom teacher. I remember very well the Bible classes he taught every morning. We enjoyed different stories from the Bible cleverly told by the teacher. I was fascinated to hear these stories because I identified with each of the biblical characters as he narrated the account.

Mr. Santiago had an exceptional ability to leave one in suspense until the next day. I remember the morning he told us the story of Abraham when he went to sacrifice his son Isaac at God's request on Mount Moriah. He told us in detail how Abraham built an altar on the mountain and asked Isaac to lie down, and when Abraham raised his knife to sacrifice his son, at that precise moment, our teacher stopped the story and told us, "We'll continue tomorrow." He was a masterful storyteller; the truth is that he enjoyed his stories. The classes that followed were

English, Spanish, math, etc. We attended church in the morning. I don't remember how many times a week we went, but I know we attended every week.

Later, I thoroughly enjoyed the sixth and seventh grades. I remember enrolling in Mrs. Sonia Colón's typing class as an elective. Other elective courses included poultry farming and baking. I was the only male in the typing class, as I recall. I learned a lot, and what Mrs. Colón taught me has helped me to write documents and manage the keyboard throughout my life. For this, I am very grateful.

I fondly remember Mr. Ramón Alvarado (RIP), who taught us mathematics with a vast knowledge of this subject. I greatly appreciated and respected him and regretted his death. I am particularly grateful to his wife, Mrs. Felícita Bermúdez, who taught the science and social studies classes.

In physical education, the teacher was Mr. Ángel Alvarado, who always tried to keep us active with different sports activities. This was one of my favorite classes.

Betania promoted sports a lot, and Mr. Alvarado was skillful in motivating us. We played softball. I remember Ms. Rosado, the assistant director. She could hit the ball really hard. They also taught us to play basketball, volleyball, ping-pong, and tetherball. These sports activities were all carried out at different times. We practiced athletics a lot.

I participated in several races, including one at least three miles long in eighth grade, as part of the physical education class. They took us on a bus from the school to the curve before the Tío Pepe Restaurant in Asomante. From there, we ran as a group to Betania. Those were tremendous experiences.

I'll always remember the track and field days we celebrated. They were special days at school. One of the sporting activities I enjoyed most was the swimming lessons given in the afternoons.

15

After a long time, Mr. Alvarado was replaced by Mr. Sadot Méndez, the renowned Puerto Rican athlete who was very knowledgeable about the sport. From my point of view, his best qualities were his humility and desire to help the students.

Another highly respected teacher was Mr. David Holderread, who had extensive knowledge of poultry farming. I did not have the opportunity to be his student, but I learned from different students about his devotion to teaching and his love for this branch of agriculture.

At this time, we were very close as a group and had great camaraderie. My sixth-grade homeroom included José Luis Alonso (my best friend from that time to the present), James Álvarez, Olga Aponte, Marirosa Colón, Mark Esch, Noel Espada, Carmen Judith Falcón, Manuela García, Carmen Gisela Green, Heriberto Hernández, María Negrón, Bethzaida Ortiz, Michelle Reagan, Teresa Rivera, Vilma Rolón, Anita Rosado, Marie Santiago, Lourdes Suárez, Elizabeth Torres, and Sylvia Vázquez. Almost all of this group stayed together until the eighth grade.

The English course was taught by Mr. Ramón Nieves, who had an excellent command of this subject. He was very disciplined and strict in the classroom. I will never forget when a group of volunteers from the Mennonite Church came from Indiana to work on renovating the school around 1973. They got up very early to work, and on several occasions, mixing concrete and other aspects of the construction didn't go well for them. Mr. Nieves had a saying that he mentioned concerning this work, which I have never forgotten. It went, "early risers do not hurry the sun." The truth is that this saying was appropriate for that situation.

In seventh grade, besides those already named, our group included Pamela Cole, Madeline Hernández, Antonio Ortiz, Héctor Ortiz, Joe Ortiz (my foster brother), Luis Rodríguez, siblings Elizabeth and Gerardo Rivera, Lourdes Suárez, Elizabeth Torres, and Sylvia Vázquez.

I was a student from 1971 to 1975. During my years at Betania, the school bus would pick me up at 7:30 a.m. at the intersection of the roads to Aibonito, Barranquitas, and Coamo, known as *"El Empalme."* There was a lot of camaraderie among those of us who traveled together. We almost always sang religious songs, usually in the morning. For family reasons, my studies at the academy ended when I entered ninth grade. My parents and I moved to Cleveland, Ohio, during that first semester. At this time, the school director was Mr. Ángel R. Falcón.

Over the years, I have met some fellow Betania students. In Betania, I spent some unforgettable years as a student. Today, I recognize that the school's educational philosophy, which focused on the combination of studies, sports, and the teaching of Christian love, was an essential pillar in my development as a human being and as a professional. I will always be very grateful to the teachers who educated me with unparalleled love and devotion, ensuring that all students learned to be good people. May God bless you all—my teachers and fellow students— wherever you are!

_____

Original version in Spanish

3

MY SIX MONTHS AT BETANIA

Becky Holsinger Rand

Although I spent far less time at Betania than most students, it was nevertheless a memorable experience for me. To this day, I cherish the friendships that started at Betania and still continue, fifty-plus years later. My memories of my childhood years in Hesston, Kansas, were often of hearing "Puerto Rico" and the many associated words—La Plata, Aibonito, Betania, San Juan, MCC—not to mention the names of my parents' (Justus and Salome Holsinger) good friends and co-workers from their years in Puerto Rico.

My parents met in 1944 in La Plata, where my dad was the director of the La Plata Mennonite project, and my mother was one of the first MCC nurses. They married that same year in San Juan. As Dad always said, they had no idea how long the war would last, and he was there for the duration. With Dad already being a relatively old bachelor of 33 and Mom considered an "old maid" at 27, why wait to marry? My brother Dave was born two years later while they lived briefly in Bluffton, Ohio, followed by Don's birth in the La Plata hospital (the former chicken hatchery). Betty and I were born later in Kansas.

When Dad had a sabbatical leave in 1969 from his academic duties at Bethel College, returning to Puerto Rico became an option. My parents, older sister Betty, and I would return to Mom and Dad's beloved Puerto Rico, so he could write a book on the changes that had taken place in Puerto Rico during the previous twenty-five years. I had never visited Puerto Rico, and the thought of living in Puerto Rico was an enticing adventure! A bit scary, too, but I don't remember that being an issue. It was exciting to think of seeing the places my parents had mentioned so often.

The plan was to spend six months in Puerto Rico. In those days when correspondence was via mail, we planned where we would live (at the Aibonito VS Unit house) and for many other details, including my education. I was eager to attend Betania as a ninth grader, although the fact that I didn't know much Spanish was a concern. My parents often spoke Spanish when they didn't want us to know what they were saying, so I only knew a few words and phrases. Even the name Betania had an exotic sound, and I doubt I knew it was Spanish for Bethany.

After a wonderful summer in Puerto Rico, much of it traveling around the Island while my dad, with Mom's help, researched the changes that had taken place in Puerto Rico during the intervening two decades, I started school at Betania. I met a few future classmates and teachers over the summer, attending local churches, at the beach, and on other outings, and joining fun musical gatherings on the VS Unit porch. I am sure some, especially those at the VS Unit and in social gatherings, were not thrilled with the pesky 13-year-old, but I enjoyed it immensely.

A few of my Betania memories and experiences may be similar to those of other former students and teachers—or may be very different. School uniforms were transitioning to new fabric, so during the fall of the 1969–70 school year, uniforms were optional. Coming from a public school, I had never worn a school uniform before, so I found it enjoyable and less worrisome because I did not have to decide what to wear each day. I was among the few who often wore the handmade, green-checkered gingham jumper.

Teachers were helpful, letting me answer tests and assignments in English, and classmates also helped out. I'm sure it wasn't easy for Mr. Falcón or my home economics teacher, who knew very little English, to deal with my lack of Spanish. I discovered that I almost enjoyed algebra, as it was one class where Spanish wasn't so necessary.

Our ninth-grade science course was challenging. Learning all the Spanish terms for bones, muscles, and much more took many evening study hours. Mom would exclaim as she helped me that her science courses in nursing school weren't as difficult as Miss Rosado's class! I remember our class dissecting a rabbit and a frog. Until Betania, I had been an okay student, but I hadn't applied myself as diligently as my older siblings, who were straight-A students. The added translation and study time on many nights, usually with my mom helping me, certainly contributed to better study skills and improved grades when I returned to Kansas.

The break time each day was fun. We could buy snacks (I loved the small cans of pineapple or mango juice—what a treat!), and we girls would visit among ourselves. I missed much of the small talk and gossip, but Ellen Graber, Linda Thompson, or Glenda Pesant would translate if it were deemed worthy of taking the time to inform me. It made me empathetic to those who are hard of hearing. They likewise miss out on small talk as it's "not important," and everyone quickly moves on to the next "inconsequential" conversation.

I eventually could understand some Spanish, but speaking it well—not so much. Funny how now, so many years later, much of my sparse Spanish comes back to me when I'm in a setting where Spanish is being spoken.

The school lunches bring back other memories. I, like most students, couldn't stand the room-temperature powdered milk. I can still taste it. But the *arroz con habichuelas*! I could never get enough, and I always asked for huge helpings. The lunchroom workers probably wondered where a short, skinny girl put all the rice and beans. Classmates would complain about the lack of meal diversity, but I loved eating the Puerto Rican food every day it was served in the cafeteria. It made sense to me that leftovers weren't thrown away but were fed to pigs behind the science and math building. The pigs eventually became cafeteria food (at least, that is my memory).

Some of the Betania customs were a surprise. For example, breaking a raw egg on one's head on her birthday meant she had to deal with smelly hair the rest of the day! Evening parties at classmates' homes—Spin the Bottle comes to mind. Teasing was done in a playful, jocular way; I don't remember it as overly mean or bullying. It was common to hear, "*¡Ay que _____!*" followed by whatever appropriate Spanish word, that could be complimentary—or not.

I fondly recall art classes with Mrs. Graber, Bible and singing with Miss Alicia Kehl, and English with Mrs. Miller, which I liked, as I wasn't at a disadvantage. Also, sitting in the back of the bus to and from school on the winding, hilly roads (made more fun by my schoolgirl crushes on Fede and Bobby) and hot, sweaty outdoor PE volleyball games, where I showed my lack of volleyball experience. Miss Glick, plus other friendly Betania employees, contributed to my feeling fortunate to attend Betania.

I was sad to leave Betania and would have preferred to stay and graduate with the ninth-grade class. Leaving Betania friends and Puerto Rico was made worse by having to return to a frigid, flat, and now more boring Kansas.

After decades of having little knowledge of Betania or contact with Betania classmates, the internet and Facebook arrived, and many of the Class of 1970 were reacquainted. The class has gathered informally in Puerto Rico, and I have been fortunate to take part in recent years (pre-Covid). Spending time together again was wonderful, always with much laughter and camaraderie. Being accepted as a former classmate by those who spent many more years together at Betania shows the welcoming, loving attitude engendered by Betania.

I plan to return to Puerto Rico and visit former classmates, now cherished friends. Visiting Betania always brings back good memories and even a few emotional tears for being a small part of Betania. My time attending Betania positively impacted me, and I am grateful.

Original version in English

4

MY DAYS AS A STUDENT AT BETANIA

Héctor R. Alicea

It is with great pleasure that I accept this challenge to try to remember my days at Betania, as we all call the Mennonite school in Pulguillas. This invitation was a surprise for me, as I have been trying to contact people who studied at Betania to gather memories of the times and the people there.

When my family decided it was time for me to start school, I wasn't old enough for first grade. Back then, one had to be six years old. The kindergarten at Escuela Elemental Federico Degetau was already full, and I was too young for first grade. I was also too young to enter first grade at Betania.

What happened was that Escuela Federico Degetau admitted me to the first grade before my sixth birthday. After completing first grade at Escuela Degetau, I went to Betania and studied there from the second through the fourth grade. Some of my siblings had already attended there for a whole school year. Even though I was only six years old, I learned a few lessons that truly helped mold who I am today. I want to share some of these in this short piece. But before that, I would like to say that I was in awe at how beautiful the school's campus was!

The first lesson I learned early at Betania was that we had to take the bus from Aibonito to Pulguillas. At first, I sometimes experienced travel dizziness, and it was uncomfortable to begin a school day that way. After a couple of weeks of traveling right after breakfast, it didn't bother me anymore. Also, I learned that it wasn't fun to travel with Mr. Fernando Luis Cains, who rode the bus and was a stern disciplinarian.

The most significant impact Betania had on me was the culture shock. When I began studying there, I had to adapt to my new school quickly. I experienced culture shock because I hadn't expected to find so many American students there. Even growing up on José C. Vázquez Street, in front of the houses of the doctors, missionaries, and their families who had come to Aibonito to work at the Mennonite Hospital, I had never been in an environment where cultures were mixed in that way. I could hear some speaking English and Spanish, all in one sentence. Slowly but surely, I began to understand what I would today call "Betania Spanglish." I began to take learning English seriously and started reading everything I could get my hands on written in English.

I owe it to Betania that I became bilingual after my time there. My English teachers in other schools always attributed my English fluency to having studied at Betania. Betania planted the seed in me. Listening to American students speaking English made me curious and motivated me to learn the language.

The second lesson I learned in Betania was the importance of Bible study. I'd never opened the Bible by myself until then. Although we prayed together as a family at home, I didn't know the different books of the Bible. Some of the other students knew how to locate them in the Bible. So I decided to memorize the order of the books of the Bible, and by the time I moved to another school after fourth grade, I had learned all of them in the correct order. I remember students taking our Bibles and walking down to *La Capilla* for Bible class. I kept reading the Bible after I moved to another school. So my relationship with Christ is rooted in learning Bible at Betania.

Although I come from a family who loved baseball, I couldn't hit, catch, or throw the ball well. But in second grade, Mr. Cains, our regular teacher, also was our physical education teacher and pitcher. He threw the ball a little fast. Seeing that I couldn't hit or catch the ball, he began to teach me to hit it by saying, "*¡Mira la pelota, mira la pelota!*" ("Look at the ball, look at the ball!"). Knowing Mr. Cains' strong character, I knew I had to hit that ball! That's how I learned to hit, catch, and throw the ball. Later, I played for years on baseball teams we formed after Villa Rosales was built. Our team played against teams from El Caserio, La Uña, El Campito, and El Reparto Robles, among others. I owe learning the basics of playing baseball to my days in Betania, although at Betania, Mr. Cains used a softball. I will never forget Mr. Cains' strong character, both in regular classes and during physical education class.

One day during swimming class, before I knew how to swim, someone pushed me into the water. I didn't like it, but I learned to swim that day. So it worked out just fine for me. Thank you for the favor. Now I've taught my daughter to swim.

Other memories come to mind. I remember taking the bus home on Friday afternoons, knowing I wouldn't return to campus until Monday. I loved the campus. It was peaceful and well-kept by Don Guillo Bonilla and others. I remember when the new *comedor* was finished and opened for us to dine there. I remember the activities to raise money to buy the new bus, which I had the opportunity to ride.

I've been a missionary now in Indonesia since April 2009. Was I influenced by the Mennonite missionaries when the time came to decide to move to Indonesia? Yes, I was. It helped me draw and structure a plan for what I wanted to do and still want to accomplish for the Kingdom of God. I remembered conversations with my father, who began working with the

Mennonites in several capacities in 1943 at the Mennonite Hospital in La Plata. Their achievements gave me the faith I needed to start and develop a ministry here in Indonesia.

Original version in English

5

THE CALL THAT CHANGED MY LIFE

Dave Holderread

The day had been a record-breaking scorcher. It was late June 2021, and as the afternoon eased into early evening, a refreshing Pacific Ocean breeze finally made its way across the Coast Range mountains and caressed the sweltering valley. A small cluster of people stood silently at our pasture's edge, mesmerized by the drama unfolding before us. Two mares grazed contentedly on sun-cured grass as their turbo-charged foals, Coquí and Picaflor, raced each other with startling speed around an imaginary track. Across the way, standing as motionless as granite statues, the older colts—Fresco, Don Pepe, and Cupido—watched the newest members of the herd in their exuberant celebration of life outside of the womb.

Breaking the silence, one of our guests turned to me with a puzzled look and asked, "How in the world did you end up with Puerto Rican horses way out here in western Oregon?" "Well," I responded, "the story of our horses is closely linked to a school located high in the mountains of Puerto Rico."

In the early 1940s, my parents, Rachel and Wilbur, met and were married on the grounds of the Castañer hospital, where my mother was director of nurses and my father's Civilian Public Service assignment was to grow and procure food for the hospital. In 1945, my parents left Puerto Rico and settled in my mother's home state of Idaho, where they started their family, and my father taught vocational agriculture.

A decade later, in the middle of the night, our family of five stumbled into our new Puerto Rican home on the Ulrich Foundation's Asomante Farm. That memorable night was just a few days after Christmas in 1955. As a three-year-old, the move turned my world upside-down—or was it right-side-up?

In short order, I fell in love with being surrounded by so many friendly people, although their fast-flowing utterances left me bewildered. Living on top of the world—or so it seemed from the farm's lofty perch—made me think we had arrived in heaven, that place adults talked about so enthusiastically. The delights seemed endless: finger-sucking calves down at the dairy barn, curious horses across the backyard fence, polka-dotted guinea fowl making a racket as they scurried about, and outlandishly colored songbirds cavorting in the hibiscus hedge. With every passing day, I became more convinced that the giant fire-breathing Lockheed Constellation airplane that had carried us up through the clouds and across the ocean had miraculously deposited my family in paradise. Father managed the dairy farm, and Mother worked for the Mennonite Mission Board as a midwife and health-care nurse.

Not long after we had settled into our island home, Mother, with me tagging along, escorted my older sisters, Carolyn and Cathy, down the farm lane to Carretera 723 to await their first-day ride to Academia Menonita Betania. When the crowded student transportation vehicle arrived, I was sure it was a mobile playground. A small truck with hard wooden benches bolted to the floor was outfitted with an ingenious pipe tailgate that was lowered for students to get on or off the truck.

Eventually, the fall of 1958 arrived, and it was my turn to join the rollicking throng on the school truck. As exciting as the ride was, I learned first-hand that to avoid painful pinches, it was prudent to keep your fingers to yourself when the tailgate was hoisted up.

In my six-year-old mind, the Betania campus was an exotic mountainside village in perpetual fiesta mode. There were houses, a clinic, multiple school buildings, and tucked off in a far corner, a grand church building accessed via a magnificent labyrinthine pathway.

The natural lay of the land provided hills to run up and steep banks to slide down. There were fields for ballgames of various flavors. The multiple play yards had geometric-shaped structures that could be swung on, slid down, scurried over, and jumped off. Even a lesson on gravity that ended with a painful kerplunk and a hurried trip to the Aibonito Hospital to have a broken arm set in a cast by Dr. Ben Kenagy could not tarnish the revelry. The older boys provided festive highlights as they skillfully spun their brightly-colored tops, surrounded by admiring onlookers.

A vivid memory was when the entire student body assembled near the cafeteria, formed a long sinuous line, and paraded down to the Pulguillas Church. We filled the sanctuary to near capacity, and the slightly musty air of the edifice reverberated with enthusiastic singing.

We were all keenly aware of who the human overlord of Betania was—the benevolent and seemingly all-seeing Carol Glick. Did she ever miss anything? At least one first grader was convinced she did not! As students arrived for school in the morning, assembled for lunch at the cafeteria, or prepared to go home at the school day's end, Carol always seemed to be stationed on some prominent perch, calling out greetings and encouragement, giving hugs or a touch on the shoulder—nearly always with that signature smile spread across her face.

Anna Kay Massanari was a gem of a first-grade teacher. In my young mind, she was very tall, calm, rather quiet, and watched

29

over us students like a protective mother hen. She read to us, sang with us, gave us lessons in many subjects, and reminded us to be kind and to wash our hands and keep them to ourselves. In other words, she was a busy, patient, and courageous lady. (Years later, I learned that Anna Kay had retired from teaching first and second grades the year after our class, due to an injury sustained while playing with her students. Did our class have anything to do with this unfortunate event? Hopefully not.) I do not recall how it transpired, but during first grade I came to the conclusion that Spanish was the official language of school. This conclusion ended up being problematic in my educational life the following year.

When lunchtime arrived on the first day, I felt famished. Anna Kay arranged us in a neat line and we embarked on the adventure of hiking up the hill to the cafeteria. Upon entering, we were embraced by the enticing aroma of the food and the friendly greetings of the cooks. After the first server placed a portion of rice on my tray and I hesitated, she inquired, *"¿Quieres más?"* *"Sí, por favor"* I responded. When I arrived at the far end of the serving line, where a sweet treat was being doled out, the server automatically super-sized my portion. From that day on, Doña Venancia Ortiz and the other cooks were my good friends.

First grade flew by. Before I could understand what was happening, there were sad goodbye hugs with Anna Kay, Doña Venancia, and all my other loved ones in Puerto Rico. (As I wrote the previous sentence, my eyes unexpectedly filled with tears.) Shortly thereafter, my family was back in southern Idaho, a foreign land I hardly remembered.

When the new school year started, I was enrolled in the local public grade school. As wonderful as first grade had been at Betania, the opening day of second grade was a disaster. That afternoon my parents were summoned to the school and informed by a very grumpy teacher that their son did not speak English. They quickly understood what had happened and agreed that this school was not appropriate for me. Mother and Father then explained to their bewildered seven-year-old that English was the only language spoken at school in Idaho.

Bright and early the next morning, I was delivered to a Lutheran school located out in the scenic but very flat countryside. The tall, friendly second-grade teacher quickly put me at ease. At noon, as we stood in the lunch line, older students could be heard groaning about the canned spinach being served that day. When it was my turn, I requested a second helping of the wilted greens. With a surprised look on her face, the server ladled out another healthy portion. Lemon cake with bright yellow frosting was the sweet of the day. As I stood before the dessert server, she smiled and said, "Anybody that eats that much spinach gets two pieces of cake." "How about that," I thought. "What worked at Betania also works here." After I completed second grade our family moved again, this time to Oregon.

———

In 1970 I graduated from high school. That fall I attended Hesston College in Kansas to pursue my boyhood dream of becoming a wildlife biologist and airplane pilot. Arriving on campus, I discovered that there were four other former classmates of mine from Anna Kay Massanari's classroom at Academia Menonita Betania: Tami Birky, Joe Greaser, Bill Sears, and Steve Oyer (my school-appointed Hesston roommate), as well as another older Betania student, Chris Rodríguez.

One cold December day, I was studying in my dorm room when a friend came to the door and said I had a call from Puerto Rico on the hallway phone. My sister Carolyn was a teacher at Betania, so I figured she was the caller. Putting the receiver to my ear, the first sound I heard was the cheerful song of the *coquí*, Puerto Rico's ubiquitous tree frog.

"Hi, this is Dave," I said. "Why hello, David, this is Carol Glick calling from Academia Menonita Betania," came the response. This was a total surprise—I had not heard Carol's distinctive voice for more than 11 years. I was pretty confident that Carol was not calling about some long-ago first-grade misdeed, but then you could never be sure! Carol continued "I understand that you have experience raising livestock and poultry. We are looking for someone to start a Title I–funded vocational poultry program here at Betania. Would you be interested?" After catching my breath following her surprise proposal, I explained my situation. Upon turning 18 earlier that spring, I had applied to PAX and had received an assignment to be an agriculture development volunteer in Bolivia. This assignment would start in 1972 after I completed two years of college.

As I came to learn, Carol was persistent. She confirmed that to teach in Puerto Rico, I would need a minimum of two years of college and that 1972 was their target date for commencing the vocational classes. Carol urged me to pray about the offer and said she would keep in touch.

Since arriving at Hesston that fall, I'd had a recurring dream that left me mildly puzzled. In the land of dreams, I was teaching at a school that had a playground full of children. Then, in that foggy transitional space between dream and wakefulness, I would protest that my future assignment was working alongside subsistence farmers, not teaching at a school. Following Carol's call, I contemplated the possible connection between her invitation and these dreams.

———

Tuesday, August 1, 1972, arrived. The Boeing 707 was purring like a contented kitten as the captain throttled back the engines and swung the aircraft in low over the northern coastline on our final descent into San Juan. I sat gazing out of a starboard cabin window when I got my first glimpse of Puerto Rico in thirteen years. A warm sense of homecoming enveloped me.

Following an adventurous car ride from the airport to Aibonito, I met the Voluntary Service members who would be my housemates: VS unit leaders Cheryl and Jim Martin, their delightful young daughter Eunice, Betania teacher Christine Yoder, Mennonite Hospital nurse Elaine Ott, and *Audición Luz y Verdad* technician Delmer Schlabach.

The next morning, Jim (who taught part-time at Betania) and I headed out in a VW Bug. We drove to Asomante, past the former Ulrich Foundation dairy farm, and on to Pulguillas on Carretera 723. As Jim slowed to turn up the Betania lane, I spied Mom's old clinic and my first-grade building on the lower campus. Ascending the hill, up ahead on the left, was the cluster of flat-roofed cement houses of my childhood memories. Rolling into the parking lot, I spotted the mid-campus playgrounds and instantly recognized them as the playgrounds from my dreams at Hesston College. At that moment, I knew this was where I belonged.

The new school year would be starting the following week, and the campus was abuzz with preparations for students to return. Jim led me to the office, where we found Carol Glick. She greeted me with her mischievous grin and a warm welcome. My first thought was, "She's shorter than I remember." Her first words were, "My, you've grown up!" We reminisced, I filled out paperwork, and then we went out for a campus tour.

Carol made a beeline toward the cafeteria, saying, "There's someone who's anxious to see you." We walked through the door, and there was my beloved Doña Venancia. As we hugged, she said, "Tell your mother not to worry, you'll be well taken care of."

The day continued to gain positive momentum as Carol introduced me to the other cooks, Carmen Ana and Guillermina Reyes. Heading down the cafeteria steps, we encountered custodian Don José David, with whom I would have frequent and pleasant interactions over the coming years. Clustered near the primary classrooms were Elba de Miranda, Norma Espada, Nayda de Díaz, and María Torres, who made me feel at ease with their friendly banter.

Carol led the way up the campus hill, past rows of classrooms, meeting friendly teachers along the way, including Israel Hernández, Heriberto Santiago, Héctor Colón, and Ramón Alvarado. A brief stop under a *flamboyán* tree gave us a chance to admire the school grounds from on high.

Continuing across the top of campus, we arrived at a building tucked in behind the outdoor basketball court. Carol had mentioned that there was a classroom plus a separate laboratory/workshop. When she opened the door, the entire building was packed wall to wall with stuff. There was no space to take a single step inside. All I could do was chuckle and say, "I see what my first task will be. I'd better get started!"

As I began untangling the contents of my future classroom, three lanky lads approached and introduced themselves: Tom, Don, and Doug Eby. (They, along with their mother, Mary Jane; father, Doctor Larry; younger siblings Janette, Karl, and Jill; assorted chickens and rabbits, and a horse named Furia, all lived on campus.) "Could you use any help?" they inquired. Thus began some of the many lifelong friendships that would grow out of my years at Betania.

The amount of work required to get the poultry program facilities functional was coming into focus. Fortunately, I already had the curriculum prepared. The year before returning to Betania, I transferred from Hesston College to Oregon State

34

University. At OSU I worked at their Poultry Research Farms and enrolled in as many Poultry Science courses as my academic schedule permitted.

When the professors learned I would be starting a poultry program in Puerto Rico, they were intrigued and offered to review the curriculum. I envisioned classes that would employ the incredible diversity and beauty of the domestic avian world to introduce students to anatomy, embryology, genetics, and nutrition, along with practical management practices. The professors' main comments were along the lines of "this looks like a college-level curriculum."

Carol wasted no time introducing me to Valetta and Alfredo Bonilla and Fern and Stanley Miller. Both families were a godsend and became invaluable mentors and unparalleled supporters of the Betania poultry program.

The Bonillas graciously answered my numerous questions, helped procure supplies, and assisted with the importation of thousands of birds for the project. A bonus was having their three children, Leslie, Lucyne, and Larry in my classes.

The Millers encouraged me to conduct multi-year experiments with ducks and geese on their farm ponds, the results of which have aided development workers in many countries and helped lead me to my life's vocation. At least once a day, I or students visited the Millers' farm to observe and tend to the waterfowl.

When my chore time at Millers' farm coincided with mealtime, Stan or Fern would often invite me to join them at their table. If I hesitated, Stan's typical response was, "If you don't help us out, we'll have to eat leftovers tomorrow!" The gleam in his eyes told me it would not be a hardship to eat any of Fern's cooking, and I did enjoy their friendship and conversation, so I accepted their invitation when my schedule allowed.

Fellow VSer Delmer Schlabach was a valuable friend to Betania and me. We spent many evenings on campus, Delmer working on the new language lab and I in my classroom or laboratory/shop. When an extra pair of hands was called for, we worked as a team. Delmer's ability to solve problems—especially if they involved motors or electricity—was a wonderful gift. We also teamed up to maintain the school's swimming pool. Once we had the pool cleaned, the chemical levels adjusted, and the filter system backwashed, we felt it was our solemn duty to test the waters and take a swim!

———

As the first day of classes arrived at Betania in the fall of 1972, I wondered how many students would want to take a poultry class. To my surprise, the majority of seventh, eighth, and ninth graders enrolled. My plan was to have the classes divided fairly evenly between academic and practicum components. Because there were no facilities for raising birds, the practicum component was essentially a shop class in the beginning. Students learned the fundamentals of using hand and power tools, and then we started to build pens and accessories.

One day early on, I was assisting several students when a loud commotion erupted behind us in the shop. When I whirled around, the scene that met my eyes was of an enraged teenager waving a handsaw as he chased a fellow student in an obstacle course around the worktables. I jumped between them and declared with as much clarity as I could muster that this behavior was unacceptable and must not happen again. We had an impromptu discussion on appropriate ways to settle differences with one another. Fortunately, this was the most intense interaction I experienced as a teacher at Betania.

In late February 1973, Al Richards hiked up the hill to my classroom, introduced himself, and started asking questions about the poultry program. Al was part of a party of six couples from Fort Wayne, Indiana, who were helping out wherever needed on campus. Al and I were walking through the workshop, looking at the projects that students were working on, when Al handed me a check for $200, with instructions to use it to buy hand tools so the students could work more efficiently.

That Saturday evening, I caught a ride with David Helmuth to Botijas, where we spent the night with VSers Cindy and Earl Toman. David gave the Sunday morning sermon at the Botijas carport church, where I assisted on Sundays. Early Monday morning Earl (who also worked at Betania) and I drove to San Juan on a buying trip for the school, including much-needed hand tools, thanks to the generosity of Mr. Richards.

If my memory serves me well, there were nine children of María Luisa and Raúl Espada at Betania in 1972–73: Teacher Norma and students Samuel, Wilma, David, Noel, Mervin, Melba, Bery, and Neftalí. (Gadiel would be in kindergarten the following year.) The Espadas showed me great kindness from the start and made me feel like part of their family. One day in December 1972, I was told to come to their house right away. When I arrived, they presented me with seven newly hatched chicks: three blacks, two bright reds, one blue, and one green. The poultry classroom thus acquired its first mascots—dye-enhanced at that!

As I interacted with a growing number of people on the Island involved with poultry, it became clear that many Puerto Ricans enjoyed raising their own fowl for aesthetic or utility purposes. However, a stumbling block for owners of small flocks was the prevalence of avian diseases and parasites. Whereas commercial growers used carefully crafted vaccinations and medication protocols to protect their mega flocks, these protective measures were not as readily available to the home flock owner. Thus an idea was hatched. As part of the research component of the

Betania poultry programs, we would study the comparative adaptability and natural hardiness of diverse domestic avian species and breeds within species.

Once sufficient infrastructure was in place, the avian importations commenced. Chickens, quail, pheasants, guinea fowl, turkeys, peafowl, pigeons, doves, ducks, and geese were acquired. Over 100 breeds were raised and compared for hardiness, disease and parasite resistance, productivity, and adaptability to the Island's climate. In the ensuing decades, information collected from this study, which was one of the largest ever undertaken, has been used by development workers and small flock owners worldwide.

As the avian population on campus surpassed that of the humans, my students declared that the poultry program needed a proper name. After robust debate, the consensus moniker they arrived at was "Avilandia." A fun project in the shop resulted in a fine sign that was designed and fabricated by several of the students and installed at the entrance of the school grounds.

———

Shortly after my arrival in Puerto Rico in 1972, Delmer Schlabach and I were dinner guests at Esther Rose and Dr. Ron Graber's home, which was located near the Mennonite Hospital in Aibonito. Once the culinary delights had been enjoyed, Ron announced that there was something he wanted to show Delmer and me. After making the short jaunt to the hospital, we were strolling down a hallway when Ron stopped in front of the closed door of what appeared to be a storage closet. With a mischievous grin, Ron opened the door to reveal a cozy, fully equipped photographer's darkroom and announced, "You are welcome to use it."

Both Delmer and I were amateur photographers, so this unexpected development put an extra bounce in our steps as we made our way back to the Grabers' house. Carol Glick had already asked if I would document activities and events at Betania on film. Now with Ron's generous offer, the possibilities were enhanced. Using his sleuthing skills, Delmer located a source for purchasing photography supplies in bulk. With reusable film cartridges and hundred-foot lengths of film in hand, we could roll our film at a reasonable price. And with access to a dark room, it was possible to take photos, develop the film, and make prints in less than 24 hours.

A benefit of having a camera on campus was the way it encouraged me to pay closer attention to both ordinary and special events throughout the day. Students' interest in my picture-taking provided opportunities for impromptu discussions on photo composition, lighting, backgrounds, film options, lens length, etc. It was especially rewarding when students brought their cameras to school, and their photos were used in the yearbook. Several students asked that I take and develop, to their specifications, photos for special assignments. One future M.D. had me prepare prints of brain scans for an eighth-grade science fair project.

The yearbook committee decided that instead of using the standard student portraits (taken once a year by a professional photo service), each graduating ninth grader could choose what they would wear and where on campus they would have their picture taken. Over the years, it was a treat to see how thoughtfully the students chose their special spot! Standing next to or leaning against a tree was popular. The number of guys who chose to sit or kneel on the ground surprised me.

Some of the choices still stand out in my mind: Noemí Colón posed leaning against a playground swing. Adriano Chiesa was dapper in his stylish suit and tie as he appeared to be gazing into the future. Jorge Cartagena wanted his picture taken on the iconic steps leading down to the Pulguillas Church, the same location where—a few years later—my fiancée and I would choose to have our engagement photo taken. Rubén Falcón held his two-year-old nephew Bryan on his lap. And I haven't forgotten that Manual Colón had his portrait taken while holding one of Betania's homing pigeons!

————

Excerpts from a letter I wrote my parents on Easter, April 22, 1973:

> Here it is a quiet, peaceful Easter evening with the outdoors refreshed by long-needed rains and the many insects and frogs singing their night songs. It has been a very full and rewarding Holy Week and Easter Day.
>
> Before going any further, thank you for helping make my birthday such a happy one. The beautiful birthday card and gifts are much appreciated. Doña Venancia was tickled that you remembered her with a gift. Cheryl (our hostess) made me a beautiful chocolate cake in the form of a chicken. It was very pretty and good. Then the Espadas had me over for a birthday party which was a surprise! They had a great big cake all decorated with birds and my name. We sang and talked and played games until close to 12:00 a.m. They are real animal and plant lovers. They purchased a pair of geese and four ducklings from the school and want some pheasants as soon as we get them. We are planning on getting a shipment of 50 pheasant chickens on June 12.
>
> Because this was Holy Week, we had no classes at Betania. Monday, Tuesday and Wednesday we had a

teachers' retreat down on the beach near Juana Díaz. Really thought it was good, as it was Spirit-centered and we had some very good experiences as a group.

The 200 ducklings and 160 goslings are doing very well. Stan Miller and the Bonillas seem pretty excited about the future of these birds and are helping a lot. Bonillas are helping me look for an incubator that has trays designed for hatching all sizes of eggs. They would like the school to hatch about 200-250 ducklings, goslings, pheasants, etc. a week for them as soon as our breeding stock is in production.

One of the great joys of working at Betania was the many opportunities to interact with students of different grades throughout the school day. Their energy and enthusiasm were inspiring and contagious. In the mornings before classes commenced, at recesses and lunchtime, and after school, there were opportunities to play tag and give swing pushes to the youngest scholars, kick soccer balls, play softball, shoot hoops, or toss an American-style football with the older ones. Students would drop by my building when they had free time to work on special projects. Once we had an incubator up and running, students would drop by first thing in the morning to see what delightful new babies had hatched during the night.

Fifth grader Eduardo "Eddie" Rivera was too young to take an aviculture class, but he was a frequent visitor to my classroom in his free time. Eddie always seemed to have an idea for a special project percolating in his mind. Possibly the most intriguing experiment was his "satellite" project. A small, lightweight container was constructed in which a frog, green leaves, and a supply of insects were housed. Contact information was printed on the outside of the capsule. A half-dozen heavy-duty balloons were filled with hydrogen gas that Eddie made by dripping tinfoil strips into wine bottles that he had partially filled with liquid lye. Once the cluster of filled balloons was attached to the capsule with stout string, liftoff took place near the basketball court amongst the enthusiastic cheers of students and faculty. The airship traveled far and, amazingly, was found by a person who contacted Eddie and provided details of when and where it had landed—mission accomplished!

Early in that first year of teaching at Betania, it became clear that my students were fully capable of handling the class curriculum I had prepared. As the 1973 academic year drew to a close, the school hosted a special program for parents and friends. Teachers were asked to have students give an overview of what they had learned that year in class. When my students took their turn, the poise and incredible detail they spoke with left me stunned. I remember thinking, "I could have them teach the classes next year!" The audience gave enthusiastic and well-deserved applause, and all I could do was smile.

———

A few days after the completion of the 1972–73 academic year, I flew to Oregon for ten days to catch up with stateside family and friends, consult with the Poultry Science personnel at OSU, and procure breeding stock of Belgian Racing Homer pigeons and aerial acrobatic performing Birmingham Roller pigeons.

On my return trip to the Island, I caught a connecting flight in New York. The plane was almost full when a fellow with a chiseled physique rushed on and sat down next to me. He was carrying a duffel bag, which he carefully arranged between his feet, and then he unzipped the top several inches. Over the hubbub of the loading airliner, a familiar cooing sound was barely audible coming from within the bag. When he noticed me looking at his luggage, my new seatmate leaned in close and whispered, "pigeons." I learned that he was a professional boxer who had homes in both New York and Puerto Rico and raised fancy pigeons as a hobby. Shaking my head in disbelief, I contemplated the chances that two people would be transporting pigeons to the Island on the same flight, one as legal goods in the cargo compartment, the other as smuggled chattel, and that these pigeoneers would be seatmates to boot! We had a rollicking time sharing stories all the way to San Juan. When we said goodbye, my new friend promised to visit me at Betania.

When Betania's students returned to campus in early August 1973, the homing pigeons I had brought from Oregon in June had produced offspring ready to begin basic training. Students learned how to catch and hold the juvenile pigeons in a manner that was safe and comfortable for both bird and human. Next, the pigeons were taught that when we whistled, they would be fed. With patience and persistence, the young feathered students were coached in the skill of entering their living quarters from outside via a one-way trapdoor when they were signaled with the mealtime whistle.

Once the young pigeons were entering their quarters reliably, students carried them a little further across campus each day and let them fly back to the dovecote located near the school's office. As the feathered athletes gained endurance and were homing from all points on campus, the next step was to have students take a pigeon home after school. On arriving home, the student would write a short note, including the departure time, attach it to the pigeon's leg, and release the winged messenger for its return flight to campus. I was waiting to remove the message, record the arrival time, and provide bird feed. The next day the notes were read in class, and the flight time was calculated.

School staff and friends were then enlisted to transport the homing pigeons to locations increasingly distant from Betania, including La Plata, Cayey, Caguas, and San Juan. Using maps, students determined the straight-line distance in miles from the release point to the school. Converting miles into yards, they then calculated the air speed of the pigeons in yards per minute before converting it into miles per hour. To the surprise of many, these fast-flying couriers consistently covered the distance from San Juan to Betania in about 30 minutes despite having to gain approximately 2,500 feet in elevation on their flight home.

Along with the hands-on activities, we reviewed the long and fascinating history of pigeons (also known as doves) being used as message carriers dating back to antiquity. The biblical account of Noah, the ark, and the dove carrying an olive leaf was our starting point.

———

Personnel departures and new arrivals were common occurrences in 1973 and early 1974 at the Aibonito VS house. In July, we welcomed Betania English teacher and librarian Linda Redfield, English and Bible teacher Phil Bedsworth, and nurse Joyce Bedsworth. The Bedsworths also became unit leaders.

At the time, I was oblivious to the significance of August 5, 1973, the day Mildred Miller (Delmer's first cousin) joined the Aibonito Unit. Mil's assignment was to assist Harry and Linda Nussbaum in starting a daycare center for workers at the Aibonito Hospital. She immediately embraced the Island and its people with warmth and enthusiasm and accompanied me to a young friend's birthday party the day she arrived in Aibonito. A bona fide rural girl, Mil lent her skills to the VS gardening projects and pitched right in with my weekend avian chores at Betania and the Miller farm.

Robert Ulrich joined the Aibonito VS Unit in early 1974. Bob had barely gotten his bags unpacked before announcing his purchase of the Eby family's horse, Furia. Not wanting to be left behind, Delmer and I decided horses should also be a part of our future. Our friend Fernando Rosado became our go-to resource for all things equine. He promptly located "DaisyMae," a mare, for Delmer and her nearly grown filly for me. Just like that, the VS stables had three steeds.

When I informed my Betania students of this new acquisition, they clamored to know her name. Well, I had to admit, the filly was nameless. A "name that horse" confab was convened right then and there. In short order, I was informed that "Flecha" was her name. I was surprised and amused at the students' enthusiastic interest in my new four-legged traveling companion.

Bob, Delmer, and I worked with the horses before or after work, and it was only a short time until we were ready to venture out on exploratory excursions. Trail rides with friends and students became part of the rhythm of our Island life.

————

One day while taking a class on a field trip, I happened to glance in the van's rearview mirror at the instant a student dropped a gum wrapper out of a window. I pulled off to the side of the road and stopped. "Puerto Rico is a magnificent treasure," I told the students. "It saddens me to see its natural beauty tarnished by mindless littering." When I instructed the paper-dropper to re-trieve the gum wrapper plus four additional pieces of litter, several classmates teased him. "Okay," I declared, "*everybody* get out and pick up five pieces of trash."

I do not remember who dropped the gum wrapper out the window. However, 45 years after the incident, I did receive a heart-warming message from a former Betania student, José Alonso. He wrote:

I am a naturalist....The first time I heard the environmental perspective was in our aviculture class....I completed a BS degree in Physics at the University of Puerto Rico, then a PhD in Astrophysics from the University of Massachusetts. I returned to P.R. to teach at the University, and also worked at the Arecibo Observatory for 12 years.

In recent years I have been working with colleagues on the issue of light pollution. The growing use of LED lighting has impacted many settings, including protected natural habitats such as El Yunque, bioluminescent bays, and sea turtles' nesting shores. We are trying to measure skyglow in many locations around the Island in order to establish illumination standards that can be used by the local agencies.

———

Conducting experiments was an important component of the aviculture curriculum, both as a teaching tool and for obtaining useful information. In one study, various diets were fed to test groups of chicks. The result was that we were able to design homemade rations using easy-to-obtain ingredients that promoted growth rates and thrivability levels comparable to those of commercially prepared feeds.

A multi-generation experiment designed to illustrate some of the basic principles of genetics was popular with the students. Red Jungle Fowl (considered the wild ancestor of most, if not all, domestic chicken breeds) were crossed with the ancient and very unusual domestic breed known as Silkies. Essentially every visible physical trait of the Silkie is vastly different from those of the Jungle Fowl. Betania's Silkies had pure white fur-like feathers, a furry head crest, furry feathers on their legs, an extra toe on each foot, an unusually shaped comb on their forehead, and skin the color of dark mulberries.

The offspring produced when we crossed Jungle Fowl with White Silkies clearly revealed which physical characteristics were dominant, incompletely dominant, recessive, sex-linked, or sex-influenced in their inheritance. The students were surprised when not a single chick produced by the original cross-matings was colored like either parent. When first-generation offspring were bred together the following year, their offspring illustrated how recessive traits that disappeared in the offspring of the original cross could reappear in some of the chicks in the second generation. This type of experiment prompted a lot of discussion among the students.

One day, Valetta Bonilla contacted me at school with an urgent request: did we have room for 600–700 week-old turkey poults? Unfortunately, the poults had arrived at the San Juan airport barely ahead of a storm that had brought traffic to a standstill on much of the Island. Bonilla's courier had finally been able to get through to the airport, was loading up the young refugees, and wanted to know where to take them since the roads leading west to where the customer lived were still closed. Especially in light of all the assistance the Bonillas had given the Betania poultry program, I was eager to help them, so I said we would find housing for the little vagabonds if they could provide poultry bedding.

There was one problem—all the school's young bird pens were full. On the spur of the moment, the solution I arrived at was to clear out my classroom and transform it into a temporary turkey nursery. In response to my SOS call, Mil, who was just finishing her day's work at Plaza de Niños, came out to Betania to help me transform my classroom into a brooder facility. We stacked all the classroom paraphernalia in one corner and were rounding up available feeders and waterers when the Bonillas delivered bags of coffee-hull bedding. The thirsty, hungry, and stressed poults arrived as we were finishing filling the waterers and feeders. We dipped each of their bills in water and did our best mother-turkey impersonations to show them where the feed was. In short order, the classroom floor was a mass of eating, drinking, and, to our surprise, strutting baby turkeys. Mesmerized by the peaceful scene, we lingered longer than planned.

The next morning, as I headed up the hill to my building, Betania director Rafael Falcón called out to me from the front of the school's office. My heart jumped as it occurred to me that maybe I should have informed him about the fowl takeover of my classroom. We climbed the hill. I opened the classroom door, and as we stood there gazing at the repurposed room, Señor Falcón chuckled and declared, "That's a sight I never expected to see!"

––––––––

My original VS assignment at Betania was for two years. Encouraged by the positive responses of the students and patrons of the poultry program, I made arrangements to remain in VS and continue at Betania for a third year. Throughout the third year, both the instructional and research components of the program thrived, and I agreed to stay at Betania for a fourth year, independent of VS.

On campus, the tiny wood-framed house near the school office was tenant-free if the lizards, rodents, and termites were ignored. After a quick perusal, I informed Señor Falcón that it would suffice as my new domicile once my VS assignment concluded. Using the suspect logic of a 23-year-old male, I wrote in a letter to my parents, "I hope that one good day of labor will put the *casita* in livable conditions."

In the spring of 1975, I arranged with Mil and some of my students to care for the fowl at Betania and the Miller farm during summer break, so I could go on a quest to learn more about the old breeds of poultry that were rapidly becoming rare. Traveling to Maryland, Delaware, Virginia, Pennsylvania, and Ohio, I visited some of North America's most knowledgeable poultry breeders. Continuing west to Oregon, I worked on an ongoing research project at OSU, searched for additional rare avian specimens for Betania, and spent some time recharging my batteries. Near the end of my Oregon sojourn, while camping in the snow at an elevation of 9,000 feet in the Eagle Cap Wilderness, I decided that when I returned to Puerto Rico, I would ask Mil if she would be my life companion.

––––––––

When the noisy L1011 Jumbo Jetliner delivered me to the San Juan airport in early August 1975, Mil was waiting in the terminal to whisk me off to my new home on the Betania campus. But first, we drove to the Eastern Airline Cargo building located on the backside of the airport to retrieve the avian rarities I had collected over the summer.

When I informed the Eastern supervisor what cargo we had come for, his face lit up, and he told me that he had looked inside all six crates and every one of the "*bonitas*" was alive and well. A swarm of cargo workers crowded around as we filled out the paperwork, asking about these strange and beautiful birds. As I had done countless times over the previous three years with people from many walks of life, I told this attentive group about Betania and its aviculture program. The entire crew stood on the loading dock, waving goodbye and calling out their good wishes as we drove away.

Leaving behind the hot and humid coast, we were ascending into the refreshing coolness of the mountains on Route 1 when I told Mil that I planned to camp out in the *casita* that first night and then spend the next day fixing it up to live in. She coyly agreed my plan would work out fine.

Arriving on campus, my first order of business was greeting my next-door neighbors—Chris, Rafael, and little Bryan Falcón, and Amy, Shane, Keith, Sherril, and Ken Mullett. When I mentioned that the campus looked exceptionally green and lush, they informed me that the summer rains had been bountiful and the temperatures cool.

The next task was getting the new birds settled into their pens. Once they were fed and watered, we grabbed my luggage and headed to the *casita*. Mil allowed me to enter first, where I was met by one of the biggest surprises of my young life—refurbished and fully furnished living quarters. With nary a hint of what she was up to over the summer, Mil had fixed broken windows, repaired sagging walls, painted the *casita's* interior, made curtains, stocked the cupboards, and made up the bed. All that was left for me to do was to carry in my luggage and unpack. Oh, and when I asked if she would consider becoming my wife, Mil responded in the affirmative. Just as she had assured me, everything worked out fine!

———

Starting with my first night in the *casita*, I was enchanted by the nocturnal soundscape of the campus and surrounding countryside. Once darkness settled in, there were virtually no human noises to be heard. With its almost paper-thin outer walls, the humble hut was filled with nature's symphony that lulled me into restful sleep each night. If by chance I awoke before dawn's early light, there was a good chance of hearing a far-off rooster crow a greeting that was answered by a rooster on another hill that was in turn answered by a rooster on yet another hill. The predawn crow-in show would go on and on as I drifted off to dreamland once again.

Living on campus meant I had achieved the Betania trifecta: student, teacher, and resident. And being a resident was thoroughly enjoyable. In a letter to my parents dated Aug. 9, 1975, I wrote:

> Greetings from the inner recesses of my humble abode. The quietness of the Puerto Rican night is being pleasantly broken by the *coquí*, insects and night singing birds. With my pantry stocked, a roof over my head, a bike at my side, a horse in the corral some 10 yards away, a comfortable bed and fine neighbors nearby, what more could I ask for? In other words, I'm fine and feel good about being back at Betania.

My horse Flecha accompanied me on my move to the school premises. When Bob Ulrich finished his VS term and returned stateside, Furia joined us on campus and was reunited with his buddy, Flecha.

Having the horses on campus turned out better than I could have hoped. Many of the students showed an interest in them and kept a close eye on them throughout the school days. It was especially endearing the way the younger scholars would engulf me in a high-energy swarm as they excitedly described their latest Flecha and Furia sightings. Then, off they would scamper on their next equine reconnaissance mission. Those two horses may have been the most closely watched equines in the world!

When the school day ended and the campus emptied, Betania, the human academy, transitioned into Betania, the equestrian academy. Though the humans who participated in the equestrian activities varied daily, the hard-core regulars were the Mullett brothers—third grader Keith and kindergartener Shane—and myself. Simply put, we had a grand time horsing around!

The school grounds were a fine place to hone our training and riding skills. There were hills to ride up, hills to ride down, trees to practice riding the perfect circle around, and playground structures to weave patterns through as we rode. Behind the uppermost buildings on campus was a large flat area where we set up horse jumps. The exhilaration of riding a fleet horse as it launches itself over a four-foot-high barrier is not quickly forgotten!

Watching the young Mullett brothers' soaring confidence, rapport, and skill with the horses helped inspire my continuing interest in the physical and mental health benefits that can result from collaboration between humans and animals.

————

In January 1976, my sister Cathy and her husband Larry Passmore arrived in Pulguillas to volunteer at Betania for a half year. This was the first time Cathy had returned to the Island since completing grade five at Betania. She thoroughly enjoyed renewing old friendships, and together Cathy and Larry made many new friends.

On March 26, 1976, Mil and I were married on a glorious spring day in her parents' yard near Greenwood, Delaware. We had hoped to have our wedding in Puerto Rico, but too many family members would have been unable to attend. So, we took a bit of Puerto Rico with us in the form of gorgeous orchids from Fern Miller, which were the centerpiece decoration, and green bananas, made into yummy chips for the reception. It was a blessing that Cathy and Larry were at Betania and assisted the aviculture students in caring for the project birds while we were gone.

We returned to Betania and the *casita* for a long-term honeymoon. And on April 2nd, our dear friends in Puerto Rico gave us a marvelous reception that we will never forget! A group gift we treasure to this day is the 26 lovely quilt blocks that people designed and embroidered, depicting memorable scenes from the school and Island.

––––––––

My interest in small-scale sustainable food-producing systems blossomed as I gained experience while developing the aviculture program. As it became clear which breeds showed the greatest potential for sustainable systems, I became alarmed at how quickly some of these breeds were nearing extinction.

During my fourth year at Betania, I concluded that these endangered breeds needed to be bred in a location from which they could be shipped safely to a much wider pool of growers than was possible from Puerto Rico. With sadness, we decided to leave our cherished Island home and return to my home area in Oregon.

As the school year drew to a close in the spring of 1976 and Mil and I prepared to leave for Oregon, staff and friends of Betania made sure that we would not forget our time working and living on campus. The Falcón and Mullett families commissioned Don José David to prepare a traditional Puerto Rican feast. Carol Glick made a lovely meal for us at her home. The school board took us to a Chinese restaurant near Coamo. The next evening, we went up the hill across from the school to the Bonillas' home one last time for a delicious meal topped off by *flan de coco*. And we rode Flecha and Furia one last time, delivering them to their new home.

After many goodbyes and tearful hugs, Valetta Bonilla picked us up at the *casita* and delivered us to the San Juan Airport for our 4:30 p.m. flight to the mainland. It was fitting that, after all the assistance the Bonillas had given to the aviculture program at Betania, Valetta was the one to give us the last goodbye hugs.

As the captain powered up the engines of the DC10 jetliner and we sped down the runway on our way into the future, I could not resist the impulse to look back over the past four years. Ostensibly I had arrived in Puerto Rico to teach. In reality, my cherished students and colleagues had instructed me.

———

Early Spring 2022 … I spent the afternoon schooling several of our pure Puerto Rican colts, including Dulce Amigo. Dulcito, as we call him, is a great, great, great-grandson of Dulce Sueño, a legendary stallion I had heard spoken of with great admiration when I was a young boy living in Asomante. When I returned to our house for supper, Millie (as she is now known) had prepared one of our favorite meals: *arroz con gandules, fricasé de pollo, tostones, aguacate, pan de agua*, and *flan*. (And as the Betania cooks liked to tease me all those years ago, I'm still "*bastante flaco.*")

As we dined, there were many "do you remember?" moments as we recalled memories of dear friends, events, and places from our treasured former Island home. Thank you, Betania, for changing and enriching our lives!

———

Original version in English

6

BETANIA PERSONNEL

Leroy Yoder

Maxine and I went to Puerto Rico in June 1960, two weeks after I graduated from Goshen College. We had wanted to go into VS for one year, but the Mission Board couldn't find a place to locate us where I, as an accountant, and Maxine, as a teacher, would fit in. But they had a two-year opening in Puerto Rico at Escuela Menonita Betania. So two weeks after I graduated, we cleared out our tiny apartment in Goshen and traveled to Ohio to Maxine's folks, who took us to Cleveland. From there, we went to New York. All the VSers and Mission Board personnel flew from New York to Puerto Rico; it only cost $90 a person. When we got to New York there was an airline strike and we could not get our regular flight. So we had to hang around there. We were joined in New York by Joanne Baker, who was also going to Betania. They couldn't get all of us a flight, but finally there was an opening for two, so Maxine and I headed out. Joanne said, "You go ahead." She was a gal with a lot of spunk and bravery, so she stayed back. But she did make it the next day.

That was the beginning of our two-year assignment in VS. John Lehman met us at the airport, and we had quite a trip to Aibonito late at night. We saw dogs running and that type of thing. We spent the night in Aibonito and went to the school the next day, about a half-hour drive. We had Spanish language lessons in the morning. Nancy Kyjuk was our teacher. I had taken

German in college, so German words would come to mind when I wanted Spanish. Well, we managed. We had the afternoon to study and do other things. They had scheduled us for maintenance in the afternoon, so we worked on the roof of Betania's main building at the top of the hill. We got that taken care of, had time to study, and had meetings with John, the principal, and the teachers. One of the interesting things was that at our last teachers' meeting before the students returned, John handed out a sheet and told us, "Now here are the bad words in Spanish you should listen for."

My primary responsibility at Betania was as assistant to the principal. I handled the finances and sold school supplies, pencils, paper, and the like. So my job ranged from selling school supplies to sometimes cleaning up restroom problems. I was also one of the bus drivers. The school had two large buses and two trucks with enclosures on the back with benches for students to sit on. One of the buses brought students from Aibonito. Since we lived in Aibonito, I drove that bus and picked up students in Asomante on the way to Betania. The other bus came from La Plata. I think Royal Snyder drove that bus. One of the two trucks brought students from Coamo. Dick Burkholder, one of the VSers, lived there and drove the truck to Betania, picking up children on the way. The other truck was in Palo Hincado. Ken Egli, another VSer, drove that one and brought it with the students to the school.

One time driving home, one student wouldn't sit down, so I left him off the bus on the outskirts of Aibonito, where he lived. I never heard any repercussions from that, and we stayed good friends. I enjoyed driving the bus; you had to be careful with the curves. Once there was a pig on the road. You couldn't slam on the brakes with a load of kids, so I hit it. When you were going up the drive to Betania in the bus full of students, you had to shift into low gear and gun it to make it up the hill. We had no accidents during the time I was there.

We had a good group of children and faculty to work with. While we were at Betania, Maxine taught about eight first-grade missionary children. She also gave piano lessons.

We had our noon meals in the *comedor*. Before going to Puerto Rico, I never liked rice. The school got government surplus food, so we always had rice. It was good the way they fixed it, and I got so I really liked rice. A lot of the kids liked *pegao*. I remember seeing the cooks scrape the crisped rice out of the bottoms of the pots so the students could get their *pegao*.

John Lehman was called back to the Mission Board in Elkhart the second year we were there. Gerald Wilson was the principal the second year, so I worked with him, doing the same things I had done my first year. I felt it was a good two years; it was a good experience for us. Things ran smoothly, and we had a good group of kids and faculty to work with.

_____

Original version in English

7

THE UNSPOKEN SACRIFICE OF A DAD

Judith Falcón Marroquín

Moon Pies

My name is Judith Falcón Marroquín. I was born in Aibonito, Puerto Rico, to Ana Meléndez de Falcón and Ramón Falcón. I am the youngest of six children. Some of my memories are a little blurry, but as I think about my childhood and Betania, this is how I remember it.

When I started in first grade at Betania, my oldest brother, Rafael Falcón, taught ninth grade. The first-grade classroom was at the bottom of the Betania property. I would walk up to the ninth-grade building and ask my brother for five cents to buy a moon pie. I don't remember my parents ever sending me to school with money to buy items at the *tiendita*, but I always ended up with my moon pie because my brother would give me five cents to buy one. His students would see me coming up to the classroom, and I would stand by the window and ask for *un vellón*, and his students would laugh at me. They knew why I was standing by the window waiting for him to finish speaking. They thought it was funny, but I am not sure my brother thought it was cute. It seemed strange that my oldest brother was a teacher when I was a student, but it was an advantage because I knew where I could get some *chavos* to buy *dulces*.

Riding the Bus

From 1967 to 1976, I rode the bus to Betania every day. I loved to sit right behind the driver because I would get motion sickness if I sat in the back. I didn't understand it then, but I do now. To avoid getting sick, I had to see the road and stay focused. It seemed like a long bus drive to school, but it wasn't that far. Every morning I would walk to the bus stop and wait with my friends for the bus to arrive. If I wasn't on time and missed the bus, my parents wouldn't take me to school, so I had to make sure not to miss the bus. I did miss the bus a couple of times, and my mom and dad were not happy with me.

The drivers were very friendly and polite. They always played music to entertain us on the bus ride to and from school. As I got older, I always felt like befriending the bus driver and requesting music I liked. There were times when there was no radio playing, and we sang songs to keep ourselves entertained. One of my favorites was: "*Ella viene desde el monte sí señor, ella viene desde el monte sí señor, ella viene desde el monte, ella viene desde el monte, ella viene desde el monte sí señor.*" I can't remember the rest of the song, but I remember singing at the top of my lungs and having the best time. I am not sure if the bus driver enjoyed it as much as I did, but most of the students on the bus joined the singing every single time. It is so true that music makes the heart joyful.

Lagartijos

My fourth-grade teacher was Mr. Israel Hernández. I thought he was a little tough. He was a nice guy, but he demanded respect and hard work in the classroom. I think I was scared of him, not because I did anything wrong, but because he required us to do the work and stay focused.

I still remember one day during recess I went to the bathroom and saw a lizard (*lagartijo*) on the bathroom wall. I couldn't go while there was a *lagartijo* watching me, so I went back to the classroom. We used the bathrooms during recess. There were no bathroom breaks during class time. I had to go but held it until lunchtime because I didn't dare ask to be excused to go to the bathroom during class.

Campanas Handbell Choir

I love music but am not musically gifted. My father arranged for me to have piano, guitar, and accordion lessons. I didn't learn any of the instruments, but not because I didn't try.

I did get to be part of the Handbell Choir while I was a student at Betania. Mr. Fred Scott was the teacher, and he loved the students. I loved the practices and performances because Mr. Scott was nice and helpful to all the students. We performed at different events, and I had a great time doing it. I can't remember how many years I was part of the Handbell Choir, but I felt important and talented when we performed our musical pieces.

I am so grateful for my years in Betania and the many opportunities I had as a student there. Learning with wonderful teachers prepared me to leave home at the young age of fifteen. The experiences, relationships, and education I received were priceless. I am grateful to my parents, especially my dad, for the sacrifices he made to send me to this school. The education, experiences, and adventures I had while attending Betania were well worth every penny he paid.

_____

Original version in English

8

I TAUGHT IN THE BARRIO WHERE I WAS BORN

Ángel Luis Miranda

The Mennonites who came to Puerto Rico understood that education was a priority for their work there. They established a school at *barrio Pulguillas de Coamo* on a plot of land donated by Don Antonio Emanuelli, one of the great landowners in Puerto Rico when the Mennonites came there in 1943.

It is a coincidence that Betania was established in Pulguillas, the community where I was born. Geographically, Pulguillas is located almost in the center of the mountainous sector of Puerto Rico. It has connections to the towns of Barranquitas (telephone service), Aibonito (electricity), and Coamo (trash services). There was a clinic near the school where *purgante*, the foul-tasting medicine to cure intestinal parasites, was prescribed.

After graduating from Goshen College in 1958, I was invited by Carol Glick, the principal at Betania, to teach Spanish and social studies at the junior-high level. I taught at Betania from 1958 to 1960. It amazed me that I became a teacher in the barrio where I was born. Today the sector of Pulguillas where I was born is called El Progreso. There is a public school in El Progreso, and I never thought a private school would emerge there in 1948 through the vision of the Mennonite workers.

I stayed at my aunt's house in Pulguillas Arriba during my first year of teaching. My aunt's residence had a sign: "*Aquí se reza el santo rosario*" ("Here we pray the Holy Rosary"). My aunt was a devout Catholic all her life. Every Sunday, she would attend a little chapel way up in the mountains. She was also my godmother. Once when I visited her, she forced me to confess my sins to the priest. The problem was that I could not think of any sins to confess, but the *cura* prompted me to express them anyway.

To get to Betania, I had to walk to the closest store to get a *público*. At that time, the paved road stopped at the grocery store. That meant I had to walk in the mud for a short distance when it rained. So, going from my aunt's house to the school was quite an adventure. Hers was one of the first houses in the area built of concrete, thanks to her two sons in the army, who helped pay for it.

The second year I taught at Betania, I moved to Coamo. My aunt Felícita became very sad because that meant she had to live alone. In Coamo, I lived behind the Mennonite church with Fernando Luis Cains and Richard Burkholder, who both taught at Betania, and Samuel Rolón, the church pastor. Richard drove the pick-up truck that took about eight students from Coamo to Betania. Mr. Cains and I rode in back to watch the students.

My experience at Coamo was unique. Every day when we got back from Betania, a fellow at a nearby store had a *posillo* of coffee for each of us. For supper, we went to a *fonda*, a small restaurant, to eat rice and beans (*matrimonio*) or rice, beans, and meat (*una mixta*).

Teaching junior-high school social studies and Spanish was always a challenge. At that time, the classes had fewer than twenty students. The ninth grade had eight girls and two boys. A few students were from missionary families. Some came from the middle-class families of Aibonito, Coamo, and Barranquitas. Others came from low-income families and needed financial help. Most of the students paid attention and were eager to learn. I was very happy with the experience, even though the salary was only about $135 a month. At that time, we began the classes with prayer.

Some of our students became professionals, in some cases occupying leadership positions in the church or Mennonite institutions. Many have made significant contributions to society at large.

I am pleased to have had the opportunity to teach in a Christian school. These schools always create a better atmosphere for the whole community. The school was also instrumental in helping me find a wife. A teacher named Lora Esch came to teach at Betania through the Mennonite Voluntary Service program. However, her assignment was shortened by one year because we married in 1962, when I was no longer teaching there. The VS directors tried to convince her to finish her assignment, but it was important to us to go through with the wedding vows. Ironically, a few years later, I became the liaison person for the VS program in Puerto Rico.

My teaching experience at the Academia Menonita Betania was the first of several church-related assignments that included pastor, chaplain, counselor, and coordinator of the VS program for Puerto Rico. The Lord guided me through the whole process.

Today, in our retirement at Greencroft in Goshen, Indiana, we continue interacting with former Betania workers and students. It was quite an experience to hear how Beulah Litwiller González used to go from house to house looking for kids to attend Betania. My hope for Betania is that it will continue functioning for many, many years to come.

_____

Original version in English

9

NINE YEARS IN FIRST GRADE

Norma Espada Stoltzfus

I started at the Betania Mennonite School in the third grade in 1955. My teacher was Patricia Brenneman Santiago. I graduated from ninth grade in 1962. Then I studied at the Aibonito high school, graduating in 1965. Afterward, I studied for two years at Interamerican University in Barranquitas.

Elmer Springer asked me if I was interested in being the first-grade teacher at Betania. I accepted the invitation and he notified Carol Glick, then director of the academy, of my decision. Glick told me that I could be the new first-grade teacher.

I began teaching first grade in 1967. Three weeks into my teaching duties, the Department of Public Education came to examine my students. They did it to determine if I could continue educating the children because I only had two years of college. They came after six months to examine them again. They did this to see if I was qualified to be a first-grade teacher.

They also gave the same exams to other first-grade classes in the region. They came to Ms. Glick and informed her that the students at Bethany were more advanced and better educated than those at the other schools. All the students at Betania had scored between 90 and 100 except for one who scored 84. I received the certificate I needed to continue teaching first grade.

I only had ten students the first year. Then more and more students kept coming. One year, 45 students enrolled for first grade. I told the principal I could only manage 30 to 35 students with an assistant. She then hired Lolita Hernández, daughter of Israel Hernández, to also teach first grade.

One year the principal was asked to allow me to meet with first-grade teachers in the school district to discuss my effective teaching methods. They also visited me on other occasions to observe my classes in action.

I enjoyed teaching at the Betania Mennonite Academy for nine years, from 1967 to 1976. I left Puerto Rico in 1976 to move to Hesston, Kansas. I went there because my sister was studying at Hesston College. I recently moved back to Puerto Rico after my husband's and mother's deaths.

_____

Original version in Spanish

10

A NUYORICAN AT BETANIA

Luis González

I arrived in Aibonito, Puerto Rico, in 1968, after graduating from college. I was a volunteer under the auspices of the Mennonite Voluntary Service. My assignment was to teach seventh, eighth, and ninth graders at Escuela Menonita Betania. Soon after arriving in Aibonito, I met Betania's principal, Carol Glick. It is said that very often, first impressions are lasting impressions. In this case, the adage is true.

I recall how impressed I was with her demeanor. She projected a serious, no-nonsense attitude, which was tempered with kindness. She was straightforward about what she expected from her teachers. As time went by, it became apparent that she had an excellent handle on all matters relating to Betania. She seemed to know all the students and their backgrounds. She had an uncanny ability to analyze and successfully resolve any adverse situation that might arise with personnel or students.

Whenever possible, Carol would share some of her immense knowledge of the customs, traditions, and culture of Puerto Rico. She knew that my knowledge of these subjects was somewhat limited since I had left the Island at the age of seven. Undoubtedly, teaching was in her blood. There was clearly mutual respect and appreciation between Carol and the teachers, resulting in Betania's smooth and efficient operation. She relied on us to teach. We, in turn, relied on her to lead.

Carol's leadership and stewardship, compassion, strength, vision, and complete dedication to Betania and the community were without equal. The interactions with her and the memories generated by them are still a joy, notwithstanding the passage of more than fifty years. They allow me to reminisce about how special and significant Betania is.

The teachers at Betania, my colleagues, seemed to me to be competent educators. Now, with the advantage of hindsight and the knowledge and wisdom acquired through the years, I realize that this body of teachers was more than competent; they were highly knowledgeable, dedicated, and committed. The teachers not only did not hesitate to offer advice to a wet-behind-the-ears rookie teacher, they also were willing to teach him when the occasion arose.

I recall Mr. Israel Hernández, a very experienced and highly respected teacher, on hearing me say to someone, *"problema resolvido,"* approached me in a discreet, respectful, and seemingly apologetic manner and said, *"Luis, no se dice resolvido, se dice resuelto."* There was another time when I was conversing with him and stated that I was *"impuesto a levantarme temprano,"* and he, in his usual respectful manner, pointed out that the word *"impuesto"* used in that context was incorrect, that the proper word was *"acostumbrado."* He proceeded to enlighten me by pointing out that *"impuesto es la contribución que se le hace al Departmento de Hacienda."* These types of interactions are possible and occur when the individual cares. He cared, and his spirit of sharing was typical of the individuals at Betania.

As these examples show, Betania's ability to attract exceptional people to its staff made it stand out and thus created an enduring memory of how special a place it is.

Another notable Betania-related experience was the friendship I cherish to this day, forged with a fellow teaching novice. By recruiting this "youngster" to the teaching ranks, Betania demonstrated a sharp eye for talent; he had many of the values that make Betania stand out, e.g., dedication, commitment, and "*amor al prójimo.*"

Although he was younger, and still is, he thought of himself as my mentor and, dare I say, caretaker. He involved me in extracurricular activities such as taking me around to neighboring towns and exposing this "Nuyorican" to additional Puerto Rican customs and ways of life, not to mention food. He was kind and generous with his time. He would pick me up in the morning on our way to Betania and drop me off after school.

Ángel Rafael Falcón, a talented and caring teacher, was a true blessing. Through his guidance I was able to appreciate and navigate my memorable journey at Betania. It is not difficult to understand why this interaction with such a giving person at Betania gave rise to a lifelong friendship.

The students were another source of pleasant and positive memories experienced at Betania, which contributed to my delightful image of the school. The students were by and large respectful, socio-economically and ethnically diverse (mainlanders and islanders), and joyful.

I also noticed that the students I taught seemed to make the utmost effort to maximize their learning according to their individual abilities. Looking back, I believe that this desire for learning was encouraged by the healthy environment at Betania created by the contributions of administrators, teachers, students, and the beautiful grounds.

The fact that the students were respectful and serious about their learning did not prevent them from being mischievous on occasion. The students felt comfortable enough to tease teachers good-naturedly. I was an easy target.

I had a distinctive way of walking, a product of growing up in New York City's aptly named neighborhood of Hell's Kitchen. When some students saw me walking towards them, they would break into an exaggerated imitation of my walk and burst into wild laughter, all at my expense. There was a particular eighth grader who would imitate my Hell's Kitchen strut whenever he would see me around town. It could be seen on his face that he was enjoying the teasing.

Softball games were played often. The teams were a mix of teachers and students. The games were played amid non-stop banter, laughter, and good-natured ribbing. These moments reflected the blessed nature of Betania and its setting. These students, whom I considered special, by extension made Betania special. I believe that the combination of exceptional administrators, teachers, students, and the rural school grounds made Betania significant and unforgettable.

Betania will always be special to me. The joyful memories created during my stay have endured. That experience has blessed me with an opportunity to become friends with splendid people who, to this day, honor me with their friendship.

BETANIA: Special and Significant Indeed!

_____

Original version in English

11

AN EDUCATIONAL GEM EMBEDDED
IN THE MOUNTAINS

Rafael Falcón

"You will be going to the Mennonite school," my father, who had recently converted to the denomination, told me. At seven years of age, I had heard of the Baptists, the Methodists and the Presbyterians on the Island, but nothing about these Mennonites. Nothing. I had studied first and second grades at the Catholic school in my home town of Aibonito, had been happy with my teachers, and was making good friends. Now I was receiving this unexpected news. Immediately I began feeling a sense of instability and uncertainty, all coming from the suggestion of this unknown world. Needless to say, I had no idea then that this fortuitous decision would profoundly change my life and that of my family for several generations.

As a Student from Third to Ninth Grades (1955 to 1962)
The light blue Chevrolet truck poked its nose into the last uphill turn toward our house in the Robles neighborhood. I had never had the experience of being transported to school, having always walked to the Catholic school and before that to the Methodist kindergarten. Now, I crossed the road, and anxiously climbed up an intimidating improvised tube ladder at the back of the truck. I found a place on the hard wooden bench among the other children, who had come from La Plata. Scared, I glanced out of

the corners of my eyes at some 15 to 20 students, who were, it seemed to me, at that very moment also checking out the newcomer, me.

We passed through the town of Aibonito, and the neighborhoods of Asomante and Pulguillas, picking up several more passengers on the way. After about six miles on a rough country road with many curves, we turned off, immediately climbing a very steep incline. At the top, we came to a grouping of buildings and houses. Some of them were made of concrete while others were of wood, American style, like the ones I had seen on television in black and white. The campus was beautiful and spacious, much more so than at the other two places where I had studied. Later I learned that the school was located on ten cuerdas of land donated by a large landowner, Don Antonio Emanuelli.

Once I got to my third-grade classroom, our teacher, *Señorita* Patricia Brenneman, welcomed us and gave instructions. Her last name did not sound familiar to me. I was used to teachers with last names like Rodríguez, Torres, and García. I timidly looked around and saw many new faces, five or six of them unlike mine. These had paler complexions, light eyes, and blond or reddish hair. They had "good hair," as we used to say to refer to straight hair. The others were like me.

At that time in the Academia Menonita Betania, uniforms were not used, unlike the schools where I had previously studied. Students attended school dressed according to what families could afford, so some children needed to use clothing patched and faded from frequent use and many washes. At times I would even see a student in bare feet. This was very different from my other schools, where everyone came well-dressed and wore shoes. Maybe it was this way, I thought, because we were in *el campo*.

Betania Culture

During my years in Betania, it struck me that great importance was given to music and prayer. At that time, the piano frequently accompanied vocal singing, more so than the guitars, tambourines, maracas, and *güiros* of the surrounding Island culture. We always sang the same song of thanks before leaving for the small dining room for lunch. We referred to the song as *Padre benigno*, from the first two words of the lyrics.

Music classes were also included as part of the curriculum, where we would sing some folk songs, and even a few in other languages. I can still remember the lyrics of several of those songs. We students were participants in choirs, and would give presentations for churches and for other activities. Individual lessons in musical instruments such as the piano and the violin were also offered for a small additional cost. I remember very well my violin lessons with the teacher Martha Kanagy.

As the school was fairly new, the facilities were quite rustic. I remember having to use the rudimentary toilet where the Anna K. Massanari building now stands. At that time there were not many sidewalks on campus, and the roads were not paved. The main parking lot did not exist. At any rate, there weren't many vehicles to park then, just the three yellow buses, the light blue truck, the dark green truck, and several of the teachers' cars. Parents did not have the custom of bringing and picking up their children at that time.

Recreational facilities were limited. There were swings, seesaws, tetherballs, and an uneven ball field filled with holes. If it rained, which happened often, recreational activities were suspended. Later on, a recreation room was built where ping-pong and board games were played. The construction of the pool and basketball court came after my student days in Betania.

When talking about my student days in the school, I must mention both the dining hall and the interesting food. It was a tiny dining room then—the current one had not yet been built— which was packed with students at lunchtime. There, four busy cooks served us the customary white rice, red beans, and other canned goods.

Some of the food offerings were famous for their unpopularity with the students. Perhaps the most notable was the cold, white, and foamy powdered milk, which sent us home fighting for immediate use of the bathroom at the end of the school day. We were also expected to finish up our servings of vegetables, such as carrots, beets, spinach or canned green beans, provided by the government. These items were very different from the typical Puerto Rican cuisine of the time.

Students found ways to leave the dining room without having to consume these unpopular foods. Undesired items could slip out the door in the hem of one's pants, unchewed in the mouth, casually held in the hands, or in other innocent-looking ways without the cooks or the teachers realizing the wrongdoing. Every now and then you could see one of the cooks a little agitated as they would inspect one of the students.

My Teachers and Classmates

During my student years I had many teachers committed to Christian education. The passage of time makes one remember some more than others, but they all impacted my life in a positive way. From my time at the school, I would have to mention Anna K. Massanari, Mercedes Meléndez, Patricia Brenneman, Rose Fuentes, Fernando Luis Cains, Carlos Lugo, Ángel Luis Miranda, Richard Burkholder, Nancy Kyjuk, Heriberto Santiago, and Israel Hernández, among others. I did not take classes with some of them, but they all left a mark on me.

As for my fellow students, I can say that, some six decades later, I still have contact with many of them, and collaborate on projects with others. As you may have already noticed, good examples of this are Tom Lehman and Galen Greaser. For me, this time in Betania created friendships that have lasted a lifetime. I graduated from Betania in 1962. As the Puerto Rican says, "*Ha llovido mucho*" (It has rained a lot), but the friendships continue.

As a Teacher of Spanish and Social Studies (1968 to 1970)

"We are offering you the middle school Spanish and social studies teacher position," Carol Glick, director of Academia Menonita Betania, informed me. I had just graduated from college a few months before and was looking for a job. The Public Instruction System had offered me work in Aibonito and in several other neighboring towns. Even though I would earn a lower salary, I decided to accept the offer from my alma mater. Now I would be returning to my Betania, this time as a teacher. My original assignment was to teach seventh, eighth, and ninth-grade Spanish and social studies. I ended up teaching intermediate physical education as well. All this work for a few dollars a month.

My Students

I walked into the classroom where I had taken those very same classes barely six years earlier. The room I entered gave me a wonderful view of almost all the entire beautiful and majestic campus of my alma mater.

Among my students I saw some I knew because they attended the same Mennonite church I did in Aibonito. I recognized others because I knew their families. With others, I had no idea who they were. The principal had informed me that there were certain students who were more prone to mischief than others, and were about to be expelled. None of these adolescents described as problematic created behavioral challenges for me. I made an effort to offer them friendship, trust, and respect. This was both difficult and easy for me, largely because I was only 20 years old myself at the time, just a few years older than my students.

Today, more than 50 years later, many of my friends on Facebook are alumni of the Academia Menonita Betania. Incredible, right? In fact, in our social media chats, several of my former students still remind me of the activities we did in some of the classes. Recently one of them, with whom I had not been in communication for decades, informed me that he has always remembered the trip we made to the Las Abejas sector of Aibonito to look for Taíno artifacts. Another told me that he has some ceramic pieces in his house found on that field trip.

As Director (1973 to 1976)

"The Board of Trustees wishes to offer you the position of director of Betania," Carol Glick—the same person who had been the director when I arrived as a novice teacher in 1968—told me. It was an honor for me to be invited to continue the tradition of administrators like Carol Glick, Gerald Wilson, John Lehman, and Merle Sommers. The invitation and the challenge now would be to replace Miss Glick, an emblematic figure in the history of Betania. It would certainly be a challenge. After much evaluation and prayer, though, I accepted the invitation. I was to be the first Puerto Rican director and also the first former student of the institution to reach that a position. More challenging still was that I was only 25 years old and had no previous administrative experience. Everything seemed to indicate that the job was too big for me. Despite this, the Board of Trustees, the faculty, the student body, and the parents fully supported me.

Since my days as a student and teacher the school had developed in many ways. One of them was the enlarged and modified curriculum. Now, in addition to the traditional classes,

Betania offered special and distinctive classes such as aviculture, pastry-making, fine furniture-making, and typing. These courses replaced the traditional home economics and industrial arts courses that I had grown up with.

The aviculture course represented for me the main innovation. In this class, taught by David Holderread, students not only studied their assigned birds but also raised, fed, and tended them. Some of the birds, such as pheasants and quails, were not well known in Puerto Rico and attracted a lot of attention.

The Economic Challenges

At that time in Betania there were a number of challenges, chief among them its financial situation. By that time the assistance from missionary funds had almost disappeared. Because the school had to support itself with a modest tuition that was not enough to cover all the expenses, other ways of raising funds had to be found. The huge responsibility of managing all that fell mainly on the director, another challenge that was in addition to all the other duties of a director.

One of the ways the school used to raise funds was the traditional celebration, the *fiesta fraternal*, celebrated on Thanksgiving Day, which had replaced the auction held by the Puerto Rico Mennonite Church Convention. Hundreds of tickets were sold and the school provided tasty food and a myriad of varied activities. Almost all the proceeds were donated and the workers were volunteers. It was certainly hard work for the organizers, but the financial gains were substantial, and families had the rare opportunity to share together as a community.

In addition, the school had a well-established program of sponsors to coordinate scholarships for students who could not pay the tuition in full. Most of the sponsors were from the United States and Canada, many who at some point in their lives had some contact with the Mennonites on the Island. At the initial teaming up with a child, the school would send a photo and information about the student sponsored. Sometimes a sponsor would visit the school and would be introduced to the student they were helping out with their donations. Occasionally a family would even invite their child's sponsor to their home, and as a gesture of appreciation would prepare a typical Puerto Rican dinner, and at times an offer a small gift.

There were also other smaller-scale ways to raise funds. Chocolate bars with almonds were always a favorite fundraiser. The student who sold the most won a prize. Also during my time as director, we initiated a project where we collected large quantities of newspapers to be sold to a Ponce recycling company. In addition, the pigs that were fed with leftovers from the dining room were sold periodically.

Medical Emergencies

One of the other challenges I experienced was the managing of medical emergencies. We had no clinic on the grounds, no nurse nearby, and the closest hospital was in the town of Aibonito, nearly six miles away, over a road full of curves, people and cars. The director was the person who had to deal with these unforeseen events.

I soon learned that whenever I would hear an agitated group of students approaching my office, something striking and interesting had happened. One unforgettable memory is of a middle-school student, surrounded by a cluster of his concerned peers, who came to my office suffering from an asthma attack. I got him into my car and drove at a meteoric speed to the Mennonite hospital in Aibonito, fearing he would not survive the trip. We happened to arrive just as several injured persons from a serious car accident on the outskirts of town were being brought in. I noticed the student becoming increasingly affected as more wounded patients arrived. But when he saw one brought in who was still trapped in the car seat, he suddenly turned to me, "Mr. Falcón, let's go. I'm fine. I'm fine." The shock of these badly injured people seemed to have pulled him out of his frightening situation.

I also vividly remember the student who attempted knocking down a *guamá* fruit by throwing a piece of wood at it. Unfortunately for him, there was a rusty nail running though the wood, which went through his thumb. I tried several times to get it out amid his screams and wails, but couldn't. So to the hospital we went on a zigzagging and painful journey, I in the driver seat and my passenger in back, desperately holding onto his piece of wood.

Accidents and unexpected moments didn't just happen during daytime hours. One notable Friday was full of work, I was exhausted and anticipating the weekend to recharge my batteries. That night we went to bed very early. Suddenly around one in the morning, the noise of shouting and shattering glass woke us. I looked out our front window, and saw movement inside the school's dining hall. Our neighbor, Kenneth Mullett, who lived nearby with his family and worked in Betania, was also awakened by the ruckus. Cautiously we walked together to the building to see what was happening. Inside we encountered a stout, inebriated man, shouting at us that they had attacked us and that we were in the middle of a war. He had been able to enter the dining hall by smashing the glass entrance doors with metal chairs mistakenly left outside.

Kenneth and I looked at each other. We had a tremendous challenge. How could we get this strong agitated man off the property? In a laborious conversation with him, I was finally able to learn that he had fought in Vietnam, that tonight some colleagues had abandoned him in front of the school entrance, and that he had an aunt living in Aibonito. We offered to take him to his aunt's house and, surprisingly, he accepted the offer. So while Kenneth drove with our visitor beside him, I was in the back seat praying that he would not have another outburst. We left him where he had indicated, and never heard from him again. But yes, the expense of replacing the glass doors was a significant financial burden for the school.

Living on Campus

Living on campus was a blessing to my young family and me, as well as a challenge. Betania was a place where there was always a lot of community action. Ballgames and basketball games were almost daily occurrences. The pool was also a favorite place for activities after school, on weekends, and in the summers. Parents were constantly coming to enroll students, or resolve academic matters after workdays or on weekends. A pay phone at the entrance to the administration office attracted a constant stream of people. Once I lost my keys to the whole school. For the next couple of days, we were looking for them like crazy. I finally found them in the pocket of the robe that I had hastily grabbed when some folks arrived on a Saturday morning.

Our Faculty and Staff

I was privileged to have a faculty committed and dedicated to the mission of the school. Although the number of Mennonites on the Island was small, we were fortunate that perhaps 90 percent of the faculty at that time was Mennonite. It was also an honor to work with several emblematic teachers from Betania: Heriberto Santiago—synonymous with fifth grade; Israel Hernández—synonymous with fourth grade; and Paula Rosado de Zayas, among others.

We also had a committed and efficient staff. There were four cooks, two of whom had served *pegao* at Betania for decades— Doña Venancia Ortiz and Doña Carmen Reyes. Recently Doña Carmen shared with me that she had finally retired, after having worked in the dining hall for more than 50 years. Imagine the number of students she saw walk by as she served food onto those metal trays!

Our janitor in those years was for me the living symbol of humility and service, Don José David. I will always remember the time he apologetically approached me at the end of a school day. Almost crestfallen, he informed me that he had heard and felt a painful cracking in his arm as he was lifting a heavy garbage can. I innocently told him to take some aspirins that I gave him. However, several hours later he returned, and informed me that he could not bear the pain. So I took him to the hospital, and there it was discovered that a tendon had snapped and needed to be reattached.

The situation turned out to be more serious and rare than I had initially thought. Even for the experienced surgeon, Dr. Ronald Graber, the operation was challenging. Days later he shared with me that he had needed to consult a medical text on the procedure while he was washing his hands for the surgery.

Our Volunteers

I cannot overlook the essential contribution of Mennonite Voluntary Service. For decades this organization provided us with teachers, maintenance workers, and administrators, among others. During my years as director we had several elementary and intermediate-level English teachers, office workers, and maintenance workers.

I remember with great pleasure the groups of North American Mennonites who came every year to help us with significant campus improvements. They provided funds and free labor for the construction of sidewalks, various classrooms, the parking lot, and for the painting of buildings, among many other things. We, for our part, provided accommodations for 10 to 12 people. Several of them stayed longer than the usual two weeks, including a young man in his 20s from Ohio, and an octogenarian couple from Indiana.

As a Parent of Fifth and Eleventh Grade Students (1989 to 1990)

"You will be studying in Betania," I informed my sons as I was making plans with Goshen College for a sabbatical year on the Island. Very different from me though, they had grown up in the states of Iowa and Indiana, and did not speak Spanish very well. The older would be going to eleventh, and the younger to fifth. This meant that the high school junior would have the challenge and the gratification of reading in Spanish *Don Quijote* and other classics from the Spanish-speaking world. Meanwhile our fifth grader would have the pleasure of studying with the emblematic Mr. Heriberto Santiago, who had been already teaching in the school in my sojourns as a student, teacher, and director. Our decision was a good one. They both had uplifting and unforgettable experiences. In addition, I had the privilege of completing my list of possible Betania connections: being the father of Betania students.

Reflections

Now several decades later, and thousands of miles away from my beloved Island, I reflect on the impact the Academia Menonita Betania has had on so many of us. In its ranks are many students who have occupied significant and vital positions in our Puerto Rican society and internationally. Some of the graduates of this humble school have held positions as university professors, doctors, lawyers, businessmen, missionaries, engineers, writers, teachers, nurses, pharmacists, artisans and artists, among many others. These graduates come not only from the town of Aibonito but also from neighboring towns such as Coamo, Cayey, Barranquitas and Orocovis. They received a quality education, and without a doubt Betania has touched each of their lives in one way or another.

I cannot finish without mentioning that my beloved father's decision to send me to study in Betania did not end there. My five siblings also studied and graduated from Betania. Several of my cousins from both sides of the Falcón Meléndez family enrolled in this Mennonite institution because of its educational quality. So my father, Don Ramón "Monche" Falcón, without knowing it, opened the gate to Mennonite education for his broader family, beginning on that day in 1955 when he informed me, "You will be going to the Mennonite school."

As you may have already perceived, the Academia Menonita Betania has been a core part of my life. This educational gem embedded in the mountains of the Pulguillas neighborhood, started by Mennonite missionaries back in 1948, has significantly marked my life forever. Unquestionably, I would not be who I am today had it not been for my father's brilliant idea, and had I not passed through the ranks of Betania, singing on countless occasions: *"Amo a mi escuela Betania por su enseñar, por su ambiente saludable que me ayuda a cada instante."*

Original version in Spanish

12

BETANIA, A GREAT BLESSING

Lora Esch Miranda

In 1961 I was completing my second year as an elementary school teacher in Kalamazoo, Michigan, when I felt God's call to go into Voluntary Service. Having inquired about places needing teachers, I was told about Newfoundland and Puerto Rico. Should I go north or south? I got another call from the administration of Voluntary Service saying that the need was more urgent in Puerto Rico. While attending a church service, I felt Puerto Rico should be my choice, so I said yes, I would go, thinking I was to teach English. I don't remember exactly when I was told that a first-grade teacher had not been found, and since I knew (a little) more Spanish than the other VSers, I would be assigned to first grade. What a surprise! Though feeling inadequate, I accepted.

When I arrived at Betania, I had to begin learning about a different culture. So many hospitable, forgiving, resourceful, resilient, wonderful people helped me adapt and learn about their environment and culture. Fortunately, I had a teacher's aide, Carmen Aurelia Colón, who interpreted when my students didn't understand my Spanish. Also, my housemate and co-worker, Leticia Jiménez, helped by checking the Spanish of my lesson plans. Miss Mercedes Meléndez was the second-grade teacher in the classroom next to mine. She was very encouraging and helpful when I was struggling or unaware of how things were done in a culture new to me. I am grateful to Betania for opening my eyes, my mind, and my heart to the beautiful culture and people of Puerto Rico. I have always believed that I learned more that year than those first graders. I hope I was able to help them grow and learn in some way.

During that school year, I had the opportunity to socialize with other VSers and Puerto Rican young people. At Betania, Ángel Luis Miranda proposed, and I became his wife. His work was in the metro area, so I completed my Voluntary Service assignment at the new Academia Menonita in Summit Hills, but I never forgot Betania.

Years later, in 1993, I was asked to become the principal of Betania and served in that role for four years. Again I felt unprepared, but I hope I did some good for students and teachers. I enjoyed teaching more than administrative work.

Betania is a place of natural beauty. From the gorgeous flamboyant tree at the top of the hill, to watching the rain come across the green mountains, to the sound of the *coquís*, its beauty inspired me. There was also the beauty the students and teachers created. I will never forget the stained-glass window in the Ana Kay Massanari building and the singing and prayers of the teachers as we met for devotions before starting the day.

One day in the students' chapel, I became very aware of the tremendous potential of the student body to bring good to the Island. It inspired me to do my job better.

Betania has always struggled financially, and there were many difficult times. Through the years, Betania has depended heavily on Voluntary Service workers from the United States. Fortunately, many of these have been experienced educators and administrators who believed in the mission of Betania and blended their wisdom with that of those from the Island to keep Betania going through good and bad times. I was blessed to have so many who helped me grow professionally and learn about the culture and beauty of Puerto Rico. It has had a positive role in the growth and vitality of the Island and the Kingdom of God. Betania has been, is now, and I hope will continue to be a blessing in the future.

—————————

Original version in English

13

ON TOP OF A HILL

Orlando Rivera

Memories are like passing clouds that come and go in a sky hidden in the deepest confines of our minds. Some memories are gray with the heaviness of a stormy day; others are bright and warm with a sense of beauty and wonder. Academia Menonita Betania is the latter for me, a wonderful place that taught me about science, literature, geography, and history. It also taught me about God, my fellow man, and community.

I consider myself blessed to have been part of a handful of children who spent nine years together, not knowing then that after Betania, our lives would never be the same. I say this because the person I am today is due in great part to those formative years that I spent at Betania.

At the top of a hill in *barrio Pulguillas de Coamo* was a light that shone brightly, lit daily by outstanding teachers and staff who went beyond simply teaching, and cared for you as if you were their child. My elementary school teachers, Srta. Lolita Hernández, Sr. Ramón Alvarado, Sr. Heriberto Santiago, and Sr. Fernando Luis Cains; and my junior high teachers Sr. Rafael Falcón, Srta. Maruchi Rosado, and Mr. Larry Yoder showered me with attention and hundreds of teaching hours. How can I ever forget? The cooking staff, led by Guillermina Reyes, who always treated me like a son, served great food and also much love. How can I not forever remain grateful?

Our principal during those years was a very special lady, Miss Carol Glick, to whom I owe much more than I could ever repay. During those years I was a curious *muchacho* who knew the route to and from her office all too well! Miss Glick would put her arm around me, look at me with kind eyes, and say, "Hello, Tito. Let's find our way back to the main road. It looks like you got a little lost in the bush." She was never impatient with me. How can I forget this love?

My classmates, who traveled through school with me from grade to grade to our last year at Betania in ninth grade, were wonderful friends. They were bright, active, kind, and caring. Although we went our separate ways after ninth-grade graduation, I have never forgotten their names or faces.

Betania was a special time and place, a season in our lives that lasted just nine years. For me, it was a perfect season, a season I have never forgotten. It was a season I look back on with fondness and love.

ATOP A HILL

Atop a hill, hidden by trees,
a bright torch I still can see,
although afar, still my heart feels
the afternoon breeze of the Coamo hills.

Atop a hill, a hidden gem,
where we conquered worlds
and learned to seek peace
and to love, for we were loved first.

Atop a hill, a light for me,
when I get lost, I remember
to look back, to look up,
don't stop 'til your goal is reached.

I am blessed to say
I am one of those Betania Boys.

_____

Original version in English

14

A FUNDAMENTAL CHAPTER IN MY LIFE

Douglas Eby

Betania was central to my experience from 1971 to 1974. These were my early- to mid-teen years, a formative time for anyone and certainly for me. Our family had moved to Aibonito so that our father, Dr. Lawrence Eby, could work at the Mennonite Hospital. All six of us siblings ended up attending school at Betania.

There are many advantages to smaller schools, where everyone knows everyone. At a smaller school no one gets away for long with problematic behaviors or a lack of engagement. The centrality of personal relationships and the importance of building community have been significant values for me my entire life. The intimacy of Betania assured the presence of both.

Being individually known was particularly important for me as I struggled with a new language—Puerto Rican Spanish—and needed some accommodation and support while learning to navigate it. The intensity of schools, with their never-ending peer pressures and rapidly evolving social dynamics, don't always go well for every student, and Betania was no exception.

However, in a smaller school that attracted mission-driven teachers, the challenges were at least more visible, more personal, and, therefore, more likely to be addressed. The commitment of many of the teachers was a great strength. I have now spent decades working in healthcare and am frequently reminded how important it is to every human to be seen, heard, and respected.

These were values instilled in me by the close relationship-based community at Betania.

The grounds and surrounding areas also held particular significance for our family, as we lived on the school grounds from 1971 to 1973. Living there came with some groundskeeping duties, which helped me learn responsibility and reliability. But most of all, it allowed us to roam the ravines and hillsides next to the school property. My brothers, sisters, and I spent endless hours exploring, building trails, and tending to various fruit-producing plants and trees. It allowed us to raise chickens, rabbits, and a horse—and to learn all that a youngster can from doing this. We were also responsible for keeping the pool healthy, which was quite an ongoing challenge. Before the internet, we greatly benefitted from roaming safely and exploring and playing imaginatively across the sizable physical area that housed Betania. I grew up a lot in those years.

It has been fifty years since we moved to Aibonito and I began attending Betania. Moving to a new place with a different language and customs can be overwhelming for many, and some of my siblings found it a less positive experience than I did. Still, for my extroverted, curious personality, it was a positive challenge that stretched me, challenged me, and, in the end, improved my confidence in my ability to take on life's challenges and thrive. Becoming comfortable in the Spanish language became a life asset that opened doors for me and helped me many times. It gave me an appreciation for different traditions, music, and food that I still treasure. I would have been lost in a large public school.

To summarize, the size of Betania, the teaching staff's attentiveness and support, and fellow students' support made the challenge manageable. It gave me the self-confidence and comfort of knowing that I was known, supported, and encouraged on my path of personal growth. It was an important three-year chapter in my life, for which I am grateful.

———————

Original version in English

15

THE EXCAVATION THAT CHANGED MY LIFE

Juan Carlos Román

My family was Catholic, and, consequently I was baptized as an infant, took first communion, and was confirmed in that religion. In May 1968, I completed the fifth grade at the Colegio Católico Sagrado Corazón in Aibonito. During the summer of 1968, the Sagrado Corazón School closed its doors. Heeding the recommendation of a friend who had her daughter in Betania, my parents decided to enroll my sister and me in the Betania Mennonite Academy for the 1968–1969 school year. My sister Marta started eighth grade that year, and I was in sixth grade.

The first thing that I liked about Betania was its location. It sat on a hill, with lots of greenery and light. This space also had the great advantage of being big enough for students to practice sports comfortably. Until then, I had never been to a school where, in addition to a nice swimming pool, there were facilities to play almost all sports: baseball, basketball, and others. At Betania, we had a field day for track and field events every year. From the beginning, all this was very attractive to me. I also liked the classrooms, which were full of light, good air, and surrounded by the same greenery.

I won't deny that the next thing I liked was the dining hall and the rich smells that emanated from it. I was chubby, a big eater, and I immediately fell in love with the delectable seasoning and the dishes that the loving cooks from Betania prepared for us. I still remember with pleasure the delicious red beans with white rice, perfectly prepared. I also really liked the government-supplied boneless chicken and turkey, how they stewed it, and the white cheese and fruit desserts. The only thing I hated was the glass of powdered white milk, served hot. They insisted we drink it, and since it was not easy to get rid of that milk, some of us resorted to pouring small amounts into each space of the metal tray and trying to hide it with bits of food. But to our dismay, they watched us closely, and when we ran to throw the scraps from the tray into the trash can, there was always a teacher on duty who had been watching us and was waiting for us at the door with another glass of milk. They did it to ensure our good nutrition, but who thinks about that at that age? It was a small price to pay, I thought, for those delicious lunches.

From the first day of my sixth grade at Betania, I enjoyed playing softball and then swimming in the pool. But more importantly, I liked my classmates from the very beginning, which made it possible to enjoy all the activities. The atmosphere of friendship in Betania was special. My classmates were almost all from Aibonito. The Mennonite volunteers at Betania came mainly from the United States. People were friendly, and we did not have to deal with artificial social distances. The great social distances I had observed in the Catholic school did not exist at Betania. Although I had not visited a Protestant church before, I did not feel uncomfortable or strange when the religious service was held and we sang those energizing hymns. In the Catholic Church, we were taught the catechism (a mixture of lessons derived from the church creed and fragments of the gospels). At Betania, I learned to use the Bible more directly. Of all this, I have mostly very good and pleasant memories. I felt at home at Betania from that first year.

Now I would like to share my most memorable moment in the three years I was at Betania, an experience that positively influenced my life and that I have never forgotten. It relates to the history class, my favorite, particularly the Puerto Rican history class that we took in seventh grade during 1969–70. Mr. Rafael Falcón was our teacher for that class. By the way, I have recently reconnected through Facebook with him after all these years. I have no doubt that he taught it with great love for Puerto Rico and its history.

As part of his class, Mr. Falcón planned a field trip to help us imagine an *areito*, the dance and song festival of the Taíno Indians of Puerto Rico. The tour complemented the lesson we were studying on Puerto Rico's indigenous period. Mr. Falcón arranged to celebrate this *areito* at Stanley Miller's residence because it was known that the vestiges of an indigenous ballpark and ceramic fragments had been found there. Since I was fascinated with history and archaeology, that news was like the announcement of a magical journey.

What happened that day is etched in my memory forever and influenced my choice of history as a career. We all dressed up a bit like Indians, each in our way, and when we got to the Millers' house, our seventh-grade class with Mr. Falcón met in a grove next to the house. There Mr. Miller told us that this was the likely location of the remains of an indigenous ball court. He explained that ceramic remains and large stones that seemed to have demarcated the space or ball court of the Indians had been found there. I was excited and delighted with this story. Then, Mr. Miller generously allowed us, after we had celebrated our *areito* and had lunch, to make some small excavations in search of indigenous artifacts.

After lunch, most of the class moved with Mr. Falcón to begin the dig on the north side of the grove, and a few of us chose other spots. I opted for the place where Mr. Miller had given us the talk, an area he had pointed to during the explanation. I knelt and prayed, "Lord, you know how much I love history and that archeology interests me. If this can be a moment that guides me to a vocation in the future, help me find something today that inspires me to walk that path."

I started digging. After about seven or eight minutes, I began to uncover a circle carved out of stone with a dot in the center. I could hardly believe it! I dug faster, more and more nervous and excited. As I enlarged the initial hole, a curved stone surface with the circle and dot fully exposed began to emerge. Finally, I managed to remove from the ground a fragment of stone split on both sides and in a curved shape. It had a carved circle and the point that was first exposed. Once out of the ground, I could see some blurred lines on both sides, geometric and decorative.

With the stone in my hands, I shouted excitedly, calling the group to come see what I had found. Everyone came running. I stepped aside to show the stone to Mr. Falcón and some classmates. Later, others in the class continued to excavate the hole I had made and extracted more remains of indigenous material, a few small stone spheres, and pottery fragments. That day others in the group found more artifacts. That little piece of indigenous history has served as an inspiration and guide. I still have it. Today I think it may be a fragment of those well-known archaeological pieces from the Taíno culture called "lithic belts," like the one in the photo at the bottom of the next page.

History has always been a north star in my life. Later, I got a bachelor's degree in history and took master's credits in archeology and anthropology. I have enjoyed working in Puerto Rico's General Historical Archives for twenty years. This institution safeguards the documents of our history, beginning with the 18th century and including the 19th and 20th centuries.

There I have had the privilege of holding original documents, keys to the history of Puerto, such as the *Grito de Lares* of 1868, the *cédula de gracia* for Puerto Rico of 1815, and original documents on the abolition of slavery in 1873. Every day I work closely with documents that bear witness to our history.

The time of Covid and quarantinegave me a space to reflect on what I experienced. That is why I wanted to take advantage of the social networks to reconnect with Professor Falcón and thank him for his great lesson and class on the history of Puerto Rico in seventh grade and that field trip long ago. It persists in my memory and took me down a path on which my love of history became a profession. Once again, taking advantage of this opportunity, I would like to say here: Thank you, Professor Falcón and thank you, Betania Mennonite Academy, for having been sowers of education and vocation.

I hope this small memory of Betania serves as a testimonial that a small seed of education planted with love and dedication in any student can bear unforeseen fruit and grow much like a tall tree. This is what happened to me at Betania.

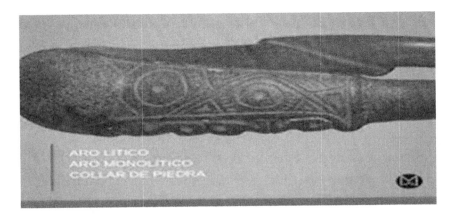

Original version in Spanish

16

MY BETANIA CONNECTION

Enrique Ortiz

My experience at Betania went through several phases. As a young man of 18, I was invited by the school principal, Carol Glick, to make leather belts and wallets to raise money for the school. I started doing that work, hoping to earn some money, but I only lasted two weeks because I didn't have the skill. I only made seven dollars, which I thought was too little. That was in 1957.

Some time passed, and in 1973 I returned to work at Betania, no longer as an employee but as a friend of the director, Rafael Falcón. He needed help to remodel his house on the school campus. So it was that my relationship with the school continued to grow. My wife, Kathy Martin Ortiz, kept the school's financial accounts.

Time is sometimes the best school in people's lives. This saying also applies to me. By 1984, I had worked in different institutions, which helped me develop knowledge and skills. At that time, the school was constructing the Anna K. Massanari building. I installed the plumbing and electricity in that magnificent building, along with Enrique Jiménez and Carlos González.

My last experience at Betania was in 1996 when I was hired and put in charge of maintenance. I did that job for five years. During those five years, with the collaboration of Frank Oyer and Earl Swartzendruber from Indiana, we worked on all the roofs of the campus buildings to prevent leaks. We also fixed up the English room, which we converted into a computer room. The computers were donated by La Academia Bautista de Barranquitas because they had bought new ones. We did all the necessary installation.

My wife, Kathy, was still responsible for the school's finances. She often came home saying, "Enrique, I don't know what will happen to the school. Payday is coming, and there is no money." But because Betania was a ministry of the Lord, He always provided.

_____

Original version in Spanish

17

BETANIA, THE SCHOOL WHERE MANY AIBONITO CHILDREN WANTED TO STUDY

Elizabeth Torres Rivera

My sisters Judith (RIP), Maritza, Emérita, and I arrived at the Betania Mennonite Academy unexpectedly. According to what our parents, Papín and Josefa Torres, told us, the Catholic school where we had studied closed from one day to the next. I don't want to think about how my parents felt. I imagine they felt lost and without many alternatives.

But I never forgot Miss Carol Glick, the director of Betania, walking into our house. She told my parents that we could study in Betania and would have help covering the tuition for the four of us (Nancy, the youngest of the five daughters, was not yet in school).

Arriving at a new school was difficult, especially for my two older sisters, Judith and Mari. For Emérita and me, it was easier because we were smaller. I got to my second-grade classroom, which in those days was in a building at the lower end of the property, and there I was received with great affection by my classmates and the teacher, Mrs. Paula Pagán.

I have wonderful and special memories of Betania. There, I learned to love and respect God, my neighbors, and nature. For me, the school is located in a paradise. We were all a family, and we worked together, parents, students, and teachers, for the good of the Academy. The values and everything positive that my teachers and staff at the Academy taught me went beyond education. All the activities, family days, school trips, and game days were great learning experiences for all of us who studied there. Everything I learned in school has helped me to cope with the experiences we face in life.

In Betania, I met wonderful people I remember with great affection who are part of my life today. In the reunions, seeing so many classmates from different classes has been a great joy. The love and respect are still there as if no time had passed.

Studying at the Academia Menonita Betania has been one of the most beautiful experiences God and life have given me. My sisters and I thank everyone who in any way helped us in our studies and helped us be part of the Betania family. The school was an essential part of our formation as Christian and professional women.

_____

Original version in Spanish

18

I WAS A CLOWN AT BETANIA

Rose Schmucker Fuentes

I earned my bachelor's degree from Goshen College and my master's degree in elementary education from Indiana University. I taught for three years in Ohio right out of college. In 1957, Valetta Sauder Bonilla and I went to Puerto Rico with our husbands, Alfredo Bonilla and Rubén Fuentes, to meet their families. While we were there, we visited Betania. Carol Glick, the principal, insisted that I come to teach. They needed a teacher for the missionaries' English-speaking children. So I began teaching seventh- and eighth-grade English at Betania. Sherilyn Hershey was one of my students, and I think twins Esther and Edith Snyder were also in that class. Classes were held in the basement of what used to be the Hershey family home and before that, Dr. Troyer's home. They paid me $75 a month at Betania. That compared to my first paycheck in Archbold, Ohio, at Zome School, which was $1,200 per year.

After two years, someone from Fort Wayne came and wanted Rubén to return to the United States to learn the diamond die business. They wanted to start a business doing that in Puerto Rico. So I only taught the middle school kids for one year at Betania. We were in Fort Wayne for two years.

We then returned to Puerto Rico, and with the birth of my daughter Joyce, I was out of teaching at Betania for a year. Little by little, I learned Spanish. The year I was away, not teaching in

Betania because I had Joyce, they hired me to teach English at the public school in the Palo Hincado neighborhood in Barranquitas. I taught fifth and sixth grades there and had sixty children in my classroom. One of them was Julio Rivera's sister. A little lady came across the mountain every day at two o'clock and brought me a *posillo* of black, black coffee.

It was probably in 1960 that I started teaching at Betania again. I took Anna Kay Massanari's first-grade class because she went to work at the Luz y Verdad radio broadcast. My Spanish was Spanglish, but I had Juana Núñez to help me with the Spanish classes. We had lots of fun. I remember that Carmen Colón, the wife of Danny Liechty and sister of Héctor J. Colón, was my assistant the second year I taught there.

My classroom was in the wooden building at the lower end of the school grounds. There were two classrooms there; Miss Mercedes Meléndez taught second grade, and I first grade. I especially remember that the windows all along the east side could be opened like barn doors, and we could look out and see the mountain across the road. Another thing I remember from our classes is that we had a unit on health, and I taught them how to make pumpkin pies. We had a huge pumpkin that grew on the patio. We cut it up and made seven pumpkin pies. I took them home at night and baked them.

In first grade, we had the animal fair, like in the class storybook, and we brought live animals to school. My daughter Joyce brought her kid goat, and Lucyne Bonilla brought her pig. The Heisers brought their horse, and it poked its head in the window. That is something I never did in the United States. That was probably the second year I taught. We also had a clown story, so I put on my clown outfit. We had a clown parade and learned some songs. We walked out of our building past other buildings, and when the other kids saw us, they joined our parade. Soon we were a long caravan going all over the school grounds.

Every December, I taught the kids in Bible class Luke 2:6-14, the Christmas story, and we acted it out. We had angels and shepherds, and we presented that little drama. To this day, I can say those verses by heart in Spanish or English.

Hilda, who later married José María Ortiz's brother, was about 12 years old when she entered first grade. She lived with her grandmother, who wouldn't let her go to school. But her grandmother finally said, "If they can teach the children to read the Bible, she can go to school." During recess, I taught her to read the Bible. She learned to read that same year, and her grandmother liked it very much.

I know that people wanted their children to be in my classes just because I knew English. For example, Dr. Colón wanted me to have her daughter in my class, but her daughter was only five years old. I told her, "Wait one more year, and I'll be glad to have her when she's six years old." That was because I started teaching my daughter Joyce when she was five years old, and that was too early for first grade. Dr. Colón and her sister had five-year-olds and said, "At least let them sit in the classroom."

Mabel Lugo taught home economics during those years and Carlos, her husband, taught fourth and fifth grades. Later Doris Snyder came, and she taught home economics, and Mr. Ramón Nieves taught Bible. A couple of years after we were there, the Graber girls came over and painted the big mural on the side of the dining room building.

One thing that sticks out in my mind from that time was a little girl named Maritza. She was from the Barranquitas area. She was very smart, but kind of sickly. She did not want to go outside for one recess, and I let her stay inside to color or do something at her desk. When I came in, she told me: "Mrs. Fuentes, I saw

Jesus in the clouds. He was very plain to me." I thought, "Well, that was neat." The following year, her family had to go to the United States because she was very ill and died of cancer. So I was very glad she had seen Jesus in the clouds a few months earlier.

One thing I remember from school is the food the government provided for the children's lunches. Carol Glick, who was the principal when I was there, insisted that all the children had to finish their food before they could leave the dining room for lunch recess. The dining room served warm powdered milk daily, and the children hated it.

I taught at Betania from 1960 to 1966, returning to Goshen in the summer of that year. Then I decided to return to Puerto Rico and taught again in Betania from 1976 to 1978. They wanted me to move to the wooden house next to the school office where Miss Meléndez had lived. It was full of rats and chickens, and I said, "There's no way, I'll go home first!" So I went to live with Valetta and Alfredo Bonilla for a while. Then Alfredo came and built the little house that is there now, between the pink house and the school office. It had three bedrooms and a living room. Lori Sommers came and lived with me in that house, and she taught physical education for a year. We had many wonderful experiences there. She was only there for a year, and when she left, I was there for one year by myself.

During this stay, I wanted to earn money to help my daughter, who was in college in the United States. So I decided to bake five pumpkin pies every night. I took orders, and I sent Lynette the money. I also helped Nelly Arroyo, Pablo's wife, who lived next door. She used to have a sandwich shop where the dining room is now. Every morning I baked a cake and sent it over. When the children got off the bus, they went to the snack shop and bought slices of fresh, warm cake. I did that for quite some time.

Also, at this time, the children from my first grade in 1960 wanted to hold a class reunion so I could meet their wives, husbands, and children. They planned a barbecue, and all I was supposed to bring was some pies because they remembered making pumpkin pies in first grade. Marcos Falcón and his brother Rubén were there, in addition to Anselmo Fuentes, who is now a doctor. Danny Espada, who now has some kind of mission outreach, was there too. Tim Nissley was another early student. Tim knew almost no Spanish when he arrived in the fall, but by January, he was joining the conversations. He learned that fast.

I remember when the pool was built. The money could have come from Harlan, Indiana, where Simon Liechty was from. A lot of money came out of that area. The pool was built in 1964 or 1965. In 1976, when I went back, Lucyne Bonilla, who had been in one of my first classes, had her birthday. They wanted to have a pool party and invited me to come to that party. Some of the guys pushed me into the pool. I was wearing a wig, and the wig floated away. I was decapitated.

That time in Puerto Rico was one of the last times I wore my clown outfit. We had had clown activities at the Waterford School in Goshen when I taught there, so I decided to take my clown outfit the second time I went to Puerto Rico. After Puerto Rico, I put on my clown outfit several times when I visited Greencroft, a retirement community near my home, and drew a few smiles from the seniors doing their therapy.

Beulah Litwiller González started Betania with Clara Springer in 1947. Beulah told me that she had just finished her college degree when they went to Puerto Rico to start the school. She asked, "Where are the students?" They said, "You have to find them." So they went up and down the mountains asking in the houses, "Is there anyone here who can't read?" That's how they ended up with twenty students in the first year. Clara didn't know much Spanish, so she taught them music. Beulah lived with Marie Snyder, who was a nurse. Decades later, we had a meeting in Puerto Rico, and they wanted Beulah to come. She was about to turn 91 years old. On that occasion, the school honored her by naming one of the school's buildings the Beulah Litwiller González Building. At that time, she was already beginning to have memory problems.

After retiring, I spent three winters with Valetta Bonilla and renewed many friendships. One was with Ángel Manuel Avilés, who was nicknamed Cusin. We had a real reunion. It was wonderful. Rose Álvarez and I had some meetings together. I had taught her, and I taught her brothers. Bobby Álvarez was my doctor when I lived there. I also met many people from Puerto Rico when Joyce ran the Rolling Scones restaurant at the Old Bag Factory in Goshen, Indiana. Many people came to the restaurant for the monthly Puerto Rican meal, and I met several who had lived on the Island.

Note: These memories are based on an interview by the editors with Rose Schmucker Fuentes.

Original version in English

19

TWO MEMORIES OF BETANIA

Elena Ortiz Hershberger

The Weather Toe

It was a beautiful Friday, *viernes social* as we used to call it. Albert Brenner, who was in charge of maintenance at Betania, decided that the grass needed to be mowed—even on a social Friday.

Lowell Hershberger, my future husband, was in Mennonite Voluntary Service at Betania. He worked in maintenance, and this included mowing the grass.

Lowell was from Ohio, where most of the terrain is flat, and the *barrancos* (ravines) of Betania were a challenge for him. He always put on his best pair of working shoes when mowing. In this instance, this is what saved his foot. He was mowing happily, as usual, when suddenly the mower quit. His foot was under the blades of the mower. He immediately saw that his shoe had two cuts and that blood was oozing out of the shoe. He quickly hobbled to the principal's office, where Mr. Merle Sommers took one look and said, "We have to get you to the hospital."

In the emergency room of the Mennonite Hospital in Aibonito, Dr. Ron Graber began by cutting off his shoe to see the severity of the damage. He found two big cuts under his big toe and stitched them up. They kept him in the hospital overnight, and he was released the next day with crutches he used for a month.

His toe healed, and now it is a good weather indicator!

Doña Venancia and *Espagueti con salchichas*

For those who don't remember, Doña Venancia was the icon of *El Comedor Escolar*. She was a fine lady who was very strict and seldom smiled. Most of the students feared her because she made us eat all the food on our plates. We didn't have a choice.

The food served in *El Comedor* was surplus from the United States government. They thought we needed a balanced diet of milk, vegetables, fruits, eggs, and pasta. The pasta was my big problem. *Espagueti con salchichas* (spaghetti and weiners), I could not eat that stuff.

Once every month, *espagueti con salchichas* was served at the *comedor*, and I would refuse to eat it. Doña Venancia would make me sit there for what seemed like hours and hours. There would be no other students in the *comedor*. There I would be, alone. No tears or anything could convince Doña Venancia to let me go. The noon bell would ring, and Doña Venancia would get tired of me and let me go.

When I was in seventh grade, Mr. Gerald Wilson was the principal, and Martha Kanagy was the math and science teacher. Mr. Wilson was a saint. Every time he saw me walking towards his office, he knew why. With a smile, he would say, "*espagueti con salchichas* again," and give me a pass for science class, and Miss Kanagy would blink and wink at me.

Well, this is the rest of the story.

I saw Doña Venancia at the Betania church in Pulguillas a few years before she passed away. I was surprised when she told me, "Elena, I am so sorry for all the times you sat alone in the *comedor* with a plate full of *espagueti con salchichas*, but those were the rules. I was just following the rules." It took a lot of courage for her to say that twenty years later.

Original version in English

20

BETANIA IS NOSTALGIA

Galen D. Greaser

Betania invokes nostalgia, but the good kind. Nostalgia takes many forms. Those who believe we live in decadent times are nostalgic for the better times of the past. "Make America Great Again" draws on this sentiment. Romantic nostalgia glorifies the past and represents it in idyllic, unrealistic terms. The melancholy version wallows in the feeling that we were well-off in the past and unfortunate now. Pathological nostalgia is obsessed with a negative comparison of past and present, becoming compulsive and depressive. Good nostalgia, for its part, views the past with a sense of gratitude and calm acceptance. It is not a matter of falsifying the past and forgetting its less favorable aspects but of remembering with gratitude and appreciation what life gave us in our youth. When we were young, we didn't have time for nostalgia. We looked at the future through a spyglass. Today, for those of us who are older, we look at life through our bifocals and a rearview mirror, sometimes clouded by longing.

In the summer of 1953, Lawrence and Annabelle Greaser moved with their family from "*La Loma*," as we called the little farm in Pulguillas owned by my grandfather, Dr. George Troyer, down to the Mennonite compound called Betania in the same neighborhood. The Betania grounds included the Mennonite church, the school and its dining hall, five houses where the church pastor and school staff lived, and a clinic. My dad had been put in charge of the church.

Our family's move to Betania coincided with my entry into the world of learning a few months later. During my first two school years, Betania was my school and also my world, the universe reduced to a hillside of ten *cuerdas* donated by Don Antonio Emanuelli, "*El Corso*," to some pacifist Mennonites carried by the ricochets of destiny to that secluded place. At the end of the school day, the place would return to its quiet peacefulness. That refuge, shielded from the frenzy, misery, wonders, and uncertainty of a vast world I barely glimpsed, contained, nevertheless, the access codes to those other worlds still distant and alien. You just had to learn them.

I entered first grade in 1953 and said goodbye to Betania in 1962. In her 1953 Christmas letter, my mother commented that I liked school but not all the food they fed us. The letter contains another fact of interest. The same year I entered first grade, my brothers Dave and Dan attended kindergarten from 8:30 to 10:30 in the morning. Sometimes there were four of us Greaser brothers at school. It seems that our little brother, Joe, two years old, would visit us until Mom tracked him down and took him back home. Living so close to school had its advantages and disadvantages for Mom.

As far as I remember, I didn't go through kindergarten. I don't know when kindergarten was added at Betania, but I do know that the school grew as I progressed, gradually adding students in nine grades. I did the full nine years, but my brothers Dave and Dan may well have been among the first, if not the first, to complete nine grades plus kindergarten. It is only a random detail, not a distinction or merit.

Each day of those first years, the smiling and friendly teachers awaited us, keepers of the secrets and keys—the alphabet and numbers—we needed to open the way to the endless universe of knowledge. Our education was classical: we learned reading, writing, and arithmetic. Nobody talked about mathematics.

To instill in us the letters, numbers, and those first simple combinations of signs that formed the foundation of our school education, the teachers used a syllabary, the blackboard, chalk, erasers, and patience. We, the apprentices, had notebooks, pencils, crayons, and empty heads. Our academic initiation was much closer to that of our parents than that of a current student to ours. The gap between the education we received and that of today's students is enormous. Those of my generation come from the pre-electronic era. We come from a pre-keyboard and pre-screen era, in other words, from the Paleolithic era, we might say. For us, there was no Sesame Street, video games, or digital tools. None of that, but we learned. One by one, we learned to form the letters of the alphabet until we could spell our names for the first time. Little by little, we added new words that we could read and write, all in the calm and attentive atmosphere that the Betania teachers maintained. The lessons were not limited to phonetics and spelling. Along with the first letters, our training emphasized the values of cooperation, respect, and courtesy, although in my case, their assimilation was not immediate or total, as you will see.

In first grade, I came across what would be a recurring factor in life: evaluations. I don't know why, but the first few times I had to review the report card with my parents, I started sobbing. I don't remember that the evaluation was bad, much less my parents scolding me, but something about it brought me to tears. For years I kept my Betania report cards, which my mother had saved for me, but they were lost along the way. I still have one, not mine, but a brother's.

The report card had two sections, one dedicated to personal and the other to academic progress. The personal progress section included categories such as punctuality, perseverance, responsibility, cooperation, honesty, courtesy, and spirituality. The "S" indicated satisfactory, the "E" outstanding, and the "✓" should improve. Until my parents managed to make me understand that the "S" did not indicate a failure, I would cry when I saw one. Blessed innocence!

The card came in a manila envelope with the following observation: "TO THE STUDENT: This report is the story of your school life. Try to get the best grades, as success depends on your effort. To succeed, in addition to instruction, you need GOOD UPBRINGING. Keep this report clean and in good condition." Inside, on the card itself, was a note to parents summarizing the purpose of all that educational effort at Betania. It said, "This report card facilitates what you as parents, and we as teachers greatly want to accomplish. We want the maximum growth and development of each child. This ideal is founded on the biblical belief that the greatest purpose of our living is to honor God, Jesus Christ, and the Holy Spirit. Only by cooperation between home, school, and the church will this goal be achieved. We believe that this report card will help us in this work."

In my case, home, school, and the church worked to put me on the right path, there is no doubt about that, and some of the good stuck to me, but in second grade, I still had a reserve of maliciousness. I have already told this in another place in the Menohispana Collection, and I won't go into details, but my misdeeds that year include: extracting from my parents' dresser, without asking permission, the pennies that were needed to win the school competition of fundraising for children in need in Africa; getting, with other tiny miscreants, under the little house of Gladys Widmer, one of the teachers who lived on the Betania grounds, to yell at her the few rude things we knew; and, at

Thanksgiving season, ripping from the classroom walls the pictures of Puritans, turkeys, and pumpkins that Ms. Widmer had hung there. Gladys was not my teacher, and the latter was an unpremeditated blowup, but no less malicious. Some regrets last a lifetime. This is one of mine. Sorry, teacher Gladys Widmer, so very sorry.

Luckily, after getting past the worst of my delinquent phase, I drifted towards more acceptable behavior, although I later made several more mistakes for which I had to pay. In one, Mr. Burkholder, the industrial arts teacher, caught me talking during class with Rafo Falcón, if I remember correctly, and punished me by making me write 250 times, "I will refrain from speaking in Mr. Burkholder's class." Then, unfortunately, I was discovered writing the 250 lines in another teacher's class, so instead of 250, it was 500! And to top it off, I got Mr. Burkholder, the one with the longest surname. I would have preferred Cains or Lugo. Then there was the time Joey "Lilito" Miller reported me to Carol Glick for bothering him on the school bus. That one earned me a couple of light slaps on my hand with a ruler before classes started that day. Considering what could have been, I think two reprimands in nine years in Betania was not too bad.

I've already mentioned Gladys Widmer. When she left Betania, they converted a small room in her empty house into a classroom for the three or four of us who took advanced English. While our classmates were learning to say "Run, Fido, run," those of us who already spoke English were given separate classes. In that little room, the teacher gave us a poem by Henry Wadsworth Longfellow, "The Arrow and the Song." The poet releases an arrow that is lost from sight and sings a song that also vanishes. Years later, he finds the arrow stuck in the trunk of an oak tree and rediscovers the song in the heart of a friend. It is from a time when poets wrote verses that even a nine-year-old could understand. I think I remember that not because I have such a good memory but because the page with the poem also had a drawing of a tree with an arrow sunk in its trunk. We learned the poem and colored the picture, which the teacher then gave us. It's another of the things I kept in my trunk for a long time and saw from time to time, but it has also disappeared.

Our education in Betania was not limited to what we learned from books. In a small dark room below the dining room, if I remember correctly, we were once shown instructional films on good table manners. They showed, I recall, the elegant way to eat spaghetti and soup. This knowledge must have been thought important for the long term and the eventuality that we might have occasion to dine with the Queen of England because, in everyday life, we found a way to get these things into our mouths without so much formality. If they had served us soup and we had eaten it as they taught us there, our classmates would have sarcastically said, "Oh, how delicate. Be careful not to break." At that age, refinement was not our thing. What would have been useful for us would have been practical advice on how to eat a mango without getting our hands and face messy. I don't think the Queen of England knew how to eat a *guamá*, a *tamarindo*, or a *quenepa*. We did!

Betania also cared about our health and hygiene. It was one thing to learn in science classes about intestinal parasites (worms, tapeworms, etc.) and quite another, the measures taken for their suppression. I remember one afternoon when they took us all out and lined us up to drink the disgusting purgative that cleaned us out. I got purged several times. Other times we were checked for lice. Another time they sent us for a general check-up with doctors from the Hospital Menonita, which was still in La Plata. All that was necessary, was fine, and came as a complement to our education. Hygiene was also on the agenda. One afternoon, the sliding doors separating the eighth- and ninth-grade classrooms were opened for a Colgate representative to demonstrate the proper way to practice dental hygiene. They may have given us a Colgate product with the idea that we would join the brand for life, which worked in my case.

Those were years when vaccines and new drugs were received with unanimous gratitude, unlike these days. I remember the day my father came to Betania to take his children to the Caserío de Aibonito, where there was a public health clinic, to get vaccinated against polio. That was in 1955 when a vaccination campaign against that devastating disease began. "Infantile paralysis," as it was also known, was dreaded by our parents. I'm sure my dad took us to get vaccinated as soon as he could, and I'm glad he did. Today polio is a thing of the past, but a vaccine has yet to be developed against today's anti-vaccine prejudices.

At Betania, they also fed us. The dining room was on a schedule; the youngest went first and the oldest last. Eating last had a great advantage: the *pegao*. After the meal, the hard-working cooks scraped the toasted residue of our daily rice from the bottom of the large pots. Doña Venancia Martínez, who deserves recognition for her long years of faithful and kind service to the students of Betania, went around distributing that delicious *pegao* to anyone who wanted some. I did not pass up my portion. Now I realize that the flavor of the *pegao* surely came from the lard used in preparing the rice. Nobody talked about cholesterol in those years, and our arteries will be paying the price today, but it sure was good.

I want to express my appreciation and gratitude to the dining room employees who put themselves out every day to feed us, although I didn't like everything that came out of that kitchen. I drank the glass of warm powdered milk they gave us every day, but I didn't like it. Some colleagues brought cocoa powder to improve the flavor, but as a boy, I didn't like chocolate, so that was not an option. What I did not eat was the traditional Puerto Rican soup, *asopao*. You had to finish everything served to you on the tray before going out to play. That was the rule. Sometimes I was alone in the dining room and missed recess because I refused to eat that "delicacy." Pumpkin and the starchy tuber, *yautía*, were not my thing. In the ninth grade, we took turns, along with a classmate, taking the leftovers from the dining room to the pigs that Betania raised on the edge of the school grounds. Some days the pigs happily enjoyed the *asopao* I despised.

I don't remember salads or fresh fruit appearing on the school menu. We would have turned up our noses at the salads, no doubt, and the fruit we had was canned. Some students claimed you would be poisoned if you ate pineapple and drank milk. Much of what we were served, I believe, was surplus from the United States Department of Agriculture given to school lunch programs. That must have been the origin of the powdered milk and the canned meats and fruits on our trays. But hey, it was what there was, and it was in no way inferior to the pizzas, hamburgers, and similar junk foods that students prefer today, which we did not have. All in all, I think we came out ahead. There was no need to talk about obesity. We were skinny. The only sugary temptation available was the delicious coconut candy that some students from La Plata brought in a jar and sold for a penny at recess time.

Once inside the dining room, before seeing what the daily menu had in store for us, we always gave thanks in the form of a song, "*Padre benigno que en el cielo estás, gracias hoy te damos por el pan que das* (Kind heavenly Father, we thank you today for the bread you give us)." I don't know when the tradition started, but I hope it's preserved. It was one of the musical moments of our day. When we were a little older, we took a music class. There we learned to sing things like "*Alouette, gentille alouette, aloutte, je te*

116

plumerai." We had no idea what we were singing, and maybe the teacher didn't either. Years later, I found out that the song is about a lark that the singer threatens to pluck, starting with its head. If we had only known. "Mambrú Went to War" was another favorite. At first, there was the question of whether he would return by Easter or on Trinity Sunday, but in the end, he suffered the unfortunate fate of so many others who have gone to war and never returned. My sister Rachel remembers that during her Betania schooldays, "Mambrú" was one of the songs they sang on the school bus.

Those of us in the choir rehearsed Christmas carols, Christmas hymns, and other sacred melodies that we presented in special programs at school and churches. Even today, I don't know what the classmates who were not in the choir did while we rehearsed. Carol Glick led the choir until Merle Sommers arrived and took over the baton. One day all the Betania students were taught a new song, "*Amo a mi escuela Betania* (I love Betania, my school)," with lyrics by Mercedes Meléndez, another teacher who left her mark in Betania, and music by Mr. Sommers. I hope that along with the "*Padre benigno*" it continues to be sung from time to time, although I fear that it may have given way to the onslaught of *regatón* and rap music.

Singing suited me better than the piano. My failure as a concert performer was resounding and definitive. Some Betania students took piano lessons, and one year a recital was organized at the school in the presence of parents and students. I don't know how I became the most "advanced" student—I assure you it wasn't because of my efforts—but as such, I had to close the program. You had to play the piece by heart, which was a problem for me because I hadn't learned the last chords well. I took the precaution of writing them down on a piece of paper and placing it on my knee, just in case. I almost reached the end safely,

117

but that's where the trouble started. I couldn't remember the final chords. I improvised some, but the only way to resolve that appalling dissonance was to look at the piece of paper and play what the composer, Beethoven, had written. Amid laughter and applause from my amused companions, I returned to my chair, crestfallen and embarrassed. Here I must, again, apologize to Beethoven, to my teacher, and to my parents, who had paid for the lessons. The piano was kept, I think, in a small room next to the director's office. The small school library was also there. There I found the first adult book I ever read, a biography of Tchaikovsky, another great composer. Today I wonder how that unexpected book got to our little school in the Pulguillas hills.

There is no school without recess, and for us, recess was playing softball. When the buses dropped us off in the morning, in the minutes before going to the classrooms, some got on the swings, others hit the tetherball, and others argued whether the Criollos of Caguas (me and several more) or the Senadores of San Juan (Rafo Falcón by himself) were the better professional baseball team. But when it was recess time, softball was our thing. In our day, there was no swimming pool, basketball court, or anything like that. We had the little softball field and a pit filled with sand when we had to practice the long jump for track and field competitions.

The softball field took advantage of a small uneven space between the elementary and middle school buildings for the infield. Along the first- and third-base lines and behind home plate were slopes where the ball kept rolling away. There were days when we spent more time running after the ball than running the bases. Finally, someone put up a backstop behind home plate, saving us some of the chasing. In left field, we had a tree with its own ground rules. If the ball landed in the tree and the player managed to catch it before it hit the ground after caroming through the branches, it was an out. If the ball touched the ground, it was a double. Once a year, we played a fastpitch softball game, attended by all the students, against the Asomante school. I played shortstop in some of those games and still remember the tension of playing fastpitch against our rival and in the presence of spectators.

One day I got my first pair of spikes, the shoes used by real baseball players. On a Saturday, I got into a *público* and went from Aibonito, where we now lived, to Betania, to try out my spikes in the ballpark. Once there, I put them on, sprinted toward first base, accelerated as I reached second base, and slid. The result was a good scare. The spikes on my right shoe caught in the dirt, and I felt my ankle twist. I got up limping and ended the session. The lesson in Betania that day was that learning sometimes hurts.

As I had barely gotten to Pulguillas, there was no point in going down so soon to catch the *público* to return home. I had to entertain myself with something else. I opted for something really stupid. I lay down on the slope beside third base and challenged the sun to a duel. Eyes wide open, I stared at the sun to see who blinked first. I do not know how long I held out, but thankfully I gave up before going blind. I don't think it was because of that, but in the eighth or ninth grade, I couldn't see the blackboard well, and they prescribed glasses for me. I was at that age when one is sensitive to what others say, and I didn't like to put them on, worried about being called "Four Eyes," but if I wanted to see the blackboard, there was no other way.

A sprained ankle was not the only injury I suffered on the Betania grounds. The first was being hit on the forehead with a bat, courtesy of Arnoldo Snyder. That drew blood, and I ran screaming to get help from Mom, who luckily was nearby. I was about six years old, and we lived in Betania, so the help was close at hand. It was fixed with Merthiolate and a band-aid. Time has

119

erased the small scar, but not the memory. Then, a wasp sting between my eyebrows made me look like an ogre for a few days. I broke my thumb playing ball at recess and my leg playing basketball. I have said that there was no basketball court in our time, but there was a basket hanging from a shed where tools were kept. That was where the leg thing happened. The Greaser brothers suffered another casualty at Betania. In the second grade, Joe, wanting to accelerate his descent down the slide, launched himself with enthusiasm from above. Unfortunately, his foot got stuck, and instead of sliding, he took flight. The landing and the resulting broken arm elicited less enthusiasm from him. The tally of accidents was not that great for the many hours we spent playing in Betania.

My broken leg had a sequel. The ninth graders had a year-end trip as a treat for completing their studies in Betania. Our class trip was to San Juan. I had a freshly broken leg and was in a wheelchair. I made the trip with my classmates, but while they toured the facilities of a newspaper and strolled through the University of Puerto Rico campus in Rio Piedras, I patiently awaited their return sitting in the van that had taken us on the outing. In the Luis Muñoz Rivera Park, I was able to get out and see the pit where a couple of very sleepy crocodiles were exhibited.

So far, I have said little about classes, studies, and teachers. It was a time when male teachers wore ties, and the women wore skirts and low heels, except for Miss Baker, who wore high heels. It's just a detail, but it says something of a time that today we would consider conservative in many social aspects. I remember not a word about sex education, although my brother Dan says he remembers a talk on the subject given by Samuel Rolón, I suppose after I had left. When a teacher named Beachy arrived in Betania, she became Miss *Playa*, for obvious reasons that seemed much less laughable then than now. The students were forbidden to have girlfriends or boyfriends at Betania. Our teachers alerted us to the ills of tobacco and alcohol, the common addictive substances of the day.

The teachers were mostly Mennonites, but not all, and none were Catholic. The administrators and half the teachers were of North American origin, Mennonites who had felt called to serve in Puerto Rico. Teachers used to be young and single. It amazes me now how little we knew about the personal lives of our teachers. I just saw on the Internet that Mister Cains, for example, was married and had children. No idea. Mister Cains was older than his colleagues, and I have a special memory of him. Of Elsa González too, for being young, pretty, and friendly, although she took a few points from me in an arithmetic exercise for not putting a comma in 1,000!

Discipline prevailed in the classrooms, and the teachers demanded our attention. I remember little of the daily routine, but the teachers taught the corresponding curriculum, and little by little, we assimilated it. The conservatism of Betania was also observed in the pedagogical method and content. We would not say that our education there was extraordinary or groundbreaking. They taught us the basics in a context that lent itself to traditional learning, with everyone at their desk and attentive to what the teacher ordered. Rigor prevailed over spontaneity. We received Bible classes, a subject that did not appear, I am sure, in the public-school curriculum. In English and music, the students of Betania were perhaps ahead of the students of the surrounding public schools; in science, maybe not. We never heard, for example, of the notion of evolution, much less of the theory itself. That subject was as discredited at Betania as the Catholic doctrine of transubstantiation. Neither one nor the other was believed.

Memory is a mystery. It erases so many events but leaves others, who knows why. I remember, for example, making a poster board with the phases of the moon in third grade. From third grade, I also remember a poem in which the right hand boasts of everything it does and of being very clever, accusing the left of being clumsy and inept. For the left, it is enough to answer that when the right hand wants its nails cut, it needs the left. Being left-handed, I liked that. Memory plays its tricks, and maybe the poem isn't exactly like that, but it's what I remember.

Around that age, we also began to write in cursive. Lessons in the Palmer Method of penmanship followed. Each letter had a correct starting point and its corresponding endpoint. That is another art on the way to extinction. Significantly, I don't remember ever using a writing instrument with ink at Betania. We never had inkwells. We used pencils. In eighth grade, we were given the task of writing a story, and mine was to personify the pencil in my hand. I had it write about the redhead who manipulated it and what he made it write. That's why I'm under the impression that we continued to use pencils even at that age, although in those years, Paper Mate had a ballpoint pen factory in Salinas I remember visiting. Surely ballpoint pens were still very expensive for the students. I suppose the hand-crank pencil sharpeners we had in each classroom have disappeared.

In fourth grade, I discovered that natural numbers are infinite, although we knew nothing about natural numbers or infinity as concepts. During part of that year, we took the class together with the fifth graders. One afternoon, while the teacher was spending time with the fifth graders, I decided to get to the last number. I wrote them down one by one until I realized there was always one more. It was clear that I was not going to be a mathematical genius, but hey, knowing how to lose is also part of education. I did learn the multiplication tables with the help of Miss Kanagy.

Seven times eight was one of the hardest to remember until she gave us a little memory trick. The result, 56, leaves the sequence 5, 6, 7, 8. Trifles embedded in memory.

When we were older, the boys were given industrial arts and the girls, home economics. They taught us to carve wooden dogs, evaluate laying hens, and disassemble an engine. One or two weeks a year, we switched. We took home economics and the girls, industrial arts. I didn't learn to cook, but I did learn something about vocabulary. When I had to put away a washcloth, I asked the teacher, "Where do I hang it?" (*¿Dónde lo güindo?*) "You don't say *güindo*; you should say *cuelgo*," she corrected me, much to the amusement of my merciless classmates.

In Ángel Luis Miranda's class, we read *El final de Norma*, with the bitter end for its protagonists, and *Marco, de los Apeninos a los Andes*, with the happy ending for Marco and his mother. "*Santa Clo va a la Cuchilla*," a story by Abelardo Díaz Alfaro, had equal parts humor and criticism. Gone is the time when parents were frightened of Santa Clo. I'm afraid they would no longer be surprised, even at the presence of Darth Vader handing out lightsabers at the Christmas party.

The days passed, and the sixth- or ninth-grade graduation day came. Dressed in our green caps and gowns, the color of Betania, we marched in straight lines to the beat of "Pomp and Circumstance" to take our seats in front of the Betania church, where the ceremony was held. On both occasions, I was chosen to give a welcome on behalf of my class. In ninth grade there were eleven of us: Josefina, Carmen, Norma, Héctor, Yuyín, Rafo, Benjamín, José Ángel, Carmelo, Ruperto, and me. I think Mister Cains wrote the sixth-grade speech. I wrote the ninth-grade speech. I resorted to one of those commonplace metaphors, graduation as the end of a chapter in the book of our lives.

Something like that. If I didn't say it then, I'll say it now. Thanks to the teachers for their dedication to the task of giving us the keys to understanding our world and the values to travel through it; to the staff who fed and cared for us; and to our parents, who sacrificed to give us a somewhat privileged educational opportunity in that environment.

From time to time, the blackboard erasers had to be cleaned. The teacher chose a student for the task. Holding an eraser in each hand, we left the room to hit one against the other hard and repeatedly. Little white clouds of chalky words and numbers that had populated our blackboard had turned to powder and now flew towards Don Antonio Emanuelli's neighboring coffee plantation, *Córcega*. If someone drinking coffee mid-afternoon in Orocovis or Cabo Rojo wondered why they suddenly began to remember the names of capitals, rivers, and planets, I can explain. They were drinking Pulguillas coffee infused with powdered knowledge courtesy of Betania.

Remembering Betania is like hitting the erasers again. Clouds of memories, images, colors, sounds, and emotions begin to emerge, tinged with our fleeting innocence and youthful optimism. Suddenly, nostalgia arrives, yearning and grateful. Nostalgia, yes, and lots of it, but the good kind.

_____

Original version in Spanish

21

MY TEACHING EXPERIENCE AT ESCUELA MENONITA BETANIA

Patricia Brenneman Santiago

Growing up, I wanted to be a librarian, not a teacher. Yet, at my mother's encouragement, or to be honest, at her insistence, I enrolled in the education program at Goshen College, Indiana, where I earned a bachelor's degree in 1953. In the fall of the same year, I began teaching about twenty-five first graders at a public elementary school in the Fruitville area of Sarasota County, Florida. For the most part, I had a good experience, except for a student from the Ringling Brothers Circus stationed in Sarasota, whom I couldn't control much.

In the summer of 1954, I was itching to visit Mennonite missionary friends in Puerto Rico, one of whom was Doris Snyder, who taught junior high students at Escuela Menonita Betania. Little did I know that during that visit I would meet my future husband, Fidel Santiago, a young Puerto Rican Mennonite about whom many people, including my father, spoke highly. Fidel always claimed that I caught his eye when I wore a yellow dress at a prayer meeting in La Plata, where we first met.

I returned to Sarasota to teach and exchanged letters with Fidel throughout the year. The visit to Puerto Rico piqued my interest in mission work, perhaps because my parents had served as Mennonite missionaries in Argentina some years earlier. I applied to the Mennonite Board of Missions for a teaching position at Escuela Menonita Betania and was accepted.

In the fall of 1955, I had my hands full teaching about thirty-five students in the combined third and fourth-grade class at Betania. I had to create my curricula. I was fortunate to be fully bilingual in Spanish and English since I grew up in Argentina. This helped me create spelling lists of Spanish words for my students to learn. I once drew a sugarcane field with ditches plowed between rows of sugarcane stalks on a large sheet of paper to illustrate the irrigation system farmers used. Classroom discipline was not my strength, but I was fortunate to have good students such as Rafael Falcón, Benjamin Colón, Tom Lehman, Eugene Hershey, and Carolyn Holderread.

In my first year of teaching, I lived with Martha Kanagy in a small house on the grounds of the Betania school in Pulguillas. Fidel and I dated during my first year in Puerto Rico. He visited me at Betania on Sundays, and I often accompanied him for worship at the Usabón congregation where he preached.

Fidel and I married on June 8, 1956 and settled in our first home in La Plata. For my second year of teaching at Betania, I took the bus with Betania students living in La Plata. Floyd Zehr drove the bus. I was assigned just the third-grade class, and it felt more manageable.

I was grateful for the support of Carol Glick, the principal at the time. I appreciated the friendship of other elementary school teachers such as Anna Kay Massanari, who taught first grade; Mercedes Meléndez, who taught second grade; Alicia Rivera, who taught fourth grade; and Carlos Lugo, who taught the combined fifth and sixth grades.

I also enjoyed my relationships with the other teachers in the seventh, eighth, and ninth grades, such as Mabel Lugo, who taught English; Martha Kanagy, who taught science, mathematics, and social studies; Doris Snyder, who taught home economics, music, and Spanish; Fred Springer, who taught industrial arts; and Leona Beachy, who came to Betania to teach advanced English classes for students for whom English was their first language.

I stopped teaching at Betania in March 1957 when I had my first child, Rolando. Alicia Rivera took over my class.

Although I did not return to teaching at Betania, both my children attended the school from first grade to ninth grade. Fidel served on Betania's school board for several years. Our family participated in the annual Thanksgiving auction, which for several years was a popular fundraising event supporting Betania.

Note: This first-person story was based on an interview that Rolando Santiago conducted with his mother, Patricia, on March 19, 2022.

_____

Original version in English

22

I FOUND PEACE

Delia C. Colón Colón

1972 was a difficult year for me. I was around 12 years old when my dad decided to enter politics. He ran for mayor of Aibonito for the New Progressive Party. It was an adventure for my parents; for me, it was a nightmare. I was in seventh grade at the Bonifacio Sánchez Jiménez School in Aibonito. I was a quiet, shy young woman with very few friends.

I found myself in the midst of the maelstrom of situations at home related to my father's political campaign. I was a young woman who stood out intellectually, but socially was another story. The bullying from some classmates and teachers was relentless. Aibonito was a stronghold of the Popular Party. The candidate who dared challenge that tradition was subject to everything from stones thrown at political rallies to insults in front of the house and on the street. Our family also received a good dose of the same.

My mother realized that my experience at school was very challenging and that it was hurting me. She decided to move two of my school-age brothers and me to Betania. She knew that we would be in a better environment and more protected, and so it was.

I came to Betania to attend the eighth grade and graduated from the ninth grade with honors in 1975. The difference was like that between heaven and earth. Thank God the harassment because of my dad's campaign and his eventual defeat finally ended. Now the task was to adapt to a new environment. Betania was a quiet place surrounded by nature that gave me a sense of peace just seeing it. My schoolmates were a heterogeneous group with very diverse ways of seeing life and behaving, and there were few of us.

Some of the teachers who had an impact on me were Mr. Sadot Méndez in English, Mrs. Sonia Colón in typing, Mr. Héctor J. Colón in social studies, Mr. José Lucena in Spanish, Mrs. Felícita Bermúdez in science, Mr. Ramón Alvarado (RIP) in mathematics, and Mr. Jorge Cartagena in baking. The ones I haven't mentioned because I don't remember them, forgive me, they also helped me a lot. I remember the school kitchen staff fondly: Venancia Ortiz, Guillermina Reyes, and Carmita Reyes. I fondly remember the school directors, Maruchi Rosado, Carol Glick, and Rafael Falcón. Mr. José David, who was in charge of maintenance, was also a beloved staff member.

I spent two very good years there. I did not stop being the shy, lonely, and somewhat sad young woman because of other events in my life, but I managed to stand out intellectually, and my spirituality grew stronger in Betania. Despite being raised Catholic, I never felt contradicted at Betania, a Mennonite school. I always felt respected for my beliefs, and I appreciate that very much.

I still have very good friendships from Betania, and I have participated in several alumni meetings in which I have had very good experiences. I hope we can continue seeing each other and sharing in the future.

After my graduation, my younger brothers continued in Betania and graduated from ninth grade. My mother saw something good in Betania to send her five children there.

I became a professional (Ph.D. in Professional Psychology) and the mother of two children who are now adults. I decided, like my mother, that the best place to educate them would be Betania. I was not wrong, thank God. Today they are good people, hard workers, and speak English fluently. One of my grandchildren was also part of Betania for a short time.

The adolescent part of me deeply appreciates the time spent in Betania because I found a lot of peace in the midst of the storm I was in. Perhaps it would have been a different story had I stayed in a place that was not for me. I eventually returned to the public school and graduated from high school, but I was strengthened by facing what I had lived through. Thank you, Betania, and all the people who accompanied me on that trip in which the motto still is "Guide me, Lord."

———————

Original version in Spanish

23

THEY CALLED ME THE CANDY GUY

Armando Rolón

I started studying at Betania at the age of eleven. I was enrolled in sixth grade. The principal at the time was Miss Carol Glick. My brothers José Luis, Juan David, and Modesto studied there later.

The monthly tuition was $6.00 per student. The Mennonite Church subsidized the balance. I contributed by washing the student transportation vehicle on Saturdays. We traveled to Betania in a blue Chevrolet 350 truck. It was modified to transport people—they made a roof, sides, benches, and tube stairs. There was another truck, this one green, for the Palo Hincado students. There was a tube ladder to get on the trucks. The ladder went up and down, with tubes sliding inside others, controlled by a lever. Many students were injured by putting their hands in the way of the tubes. The tubes stripped the skin from between the thumb and forefinger. I was one of those injured. By 1955 a large bus was acquired that left from La Plata for Betania, picking up students along the way.

My mother, an expert in making coconut candy, would prepare a glass jar with 70 to 80 pieces for me to sell at school. I couldn't sell them before lunch so the students would eat their food. I was often short of candy because I would go play and hide the jar, but some of the boys watched where I put it and would steal some candy from me while I was playing. They called me "*el dulcero*" (the candy guy). In recent years, a friend who studied in Betania at that time told me, "We stole a lot of candy from you while you were playing." Some of the teachers I had were:

Martha Kanagy: Science
Allen Kanagy: English
Mabel Lugo: English
Doris Snyder: Bible
Fred Springer: Industrial Arts
Gerald Wilson: Industrial Arts
Floyd Zehr: Industrial Arts
Marcelino Resto: Social Studies
Carol Glick: Spanish
Leona Beachy: English.

I remember the carpentry room and a vegetable garden next door. I liked all the subjects, but English and mathematics were my favorites. I don't remember the year the rec room was built. However, I vividly remember that I slipped and broke my right wrist while jumping from a wall to touch part of the roof.

The ninth-grade graduation was held at the Betania Mennonite Church. The dinner was held in a room that Torrecillas Poultry lent us. The entire building was not yet finished. The farewell was very emotional. There were a lot of hugs and tears, as we were a very close group, and it was possible that some of us would not meet again in the future.

Having studied at Betania helped me a lot with what my future would be. Today, at 78 years of age, I am proud to be a former student of the Betania Mennonite School. Blessings!

Original version in Spanish

24

I LOVE BETANIA, MY SCHOOL

Enid González

At 69 years, I'm looking back and thinking of my life, starting with my midwife-assisted birth on Padial Street and my childhood in the Pasto neighborhood of my beloved town of Aibonito. I remember my childhood, so pleasant and innocent, and my dear sister Elsa, 14 years older than me. She began attending the Aibonito Mennonite Church and preaching there.

I remember that Carol Glick made visits to our house. My parents saw in that group of missionaries a commitment and dedication to God, preaching the word of the Lord. Then my parents decided it was important that we receive a Christian education. That is how they sent my brother Leo, my sister María, and me to Betania Mennonite School. Of course, Elsa was our guide toward the Christian teaching that she was instilling in us. That is how my life as a student at the Betania Mennonite School began.

My first first-grade teacher was Ms. Anna K. Massanari. What a unique experience! The school transmitted a complete set of values to us: religion, discipline, respect, love of neighbors, development of physical, mental, and social skills, and, of course, Spanish as our first language and English as a second language. The curriculum was advanced for its time. I mention this because I taught children with disabilities for 33 years, something I take great pride in, so I have insight into the world of education.

Those missionaries came to improve the lives of the children and youth of poor communities, such as *barrio* Pulguillas. What a well-thought-out and implemented vision and mission! Of course, God guided every part of its creation. Children who could not afford tuition were charged a minimal fee. It created in us a Christian awakening that I can attest to, of which I am a product. My relationship with the school was such that it served as a guide in all facets of my life.

I was able to pass on this gift to my three children. I thank God first, then the missionaries God called to carry out such a beautiful work, known throughout Puerto Rico and in the United States. Betania is an example to follow. I currently serve communities in need in Guayama, where I reside and where I am also a municipal legislator.

As the school song says:

I love my Betania School for its teaching,
for its healthy environment,
and for its inspiration to always
fight to succeed.

Original version in Spanish

25

CLOUDS IN MY CLASSROOM
AND OTHER MUSINGS

Christine Yoder Falcón

The first time I heard of a school named Academia Menonita Betania was during a conversation over a delicious home-cooked meal. A friend, Clare Schumm, the Mennonite Voluntary Service director at the time, and his gracious wife had invited several of my college friends and me to their home after church. Eventually, knowing that I would soon graduate from Goshen College, Clare turned to me and asked about my possible next steps.

I had just returned a few months earlier from the Goshen College Study Service Trimester in Nicaragua. I was still enamored of that immersion experience outside my comfort zone that had led me into an exciting engagement with a formerly unknown language, a crosscultural reality, and new friendships. As I was in the last semester of elementary education studies, I was starting to look at options for my first placement, so my response to Clare came easily: I wanted to improve my basic knowledge of Spanish and be immersed in a crosscultural community. "Would you consider Mennonite Voluntary Service?" my host asked. "We have a couple of openings for teachers in south Texas and Puerto Rico." I chose Puerto Rico.

Classroom Joys

So it was that in August 1971 I found myself in a tiny classroom, its metal-slatted windows facing a mountain slope full of verdant plants, flowering trees, and sounds of insects, birdsongs, and *coquí* conversations. My space was the front section of a garage with a cement floor and block walls where Advanced English K–6 classes were held. My students knew English as their first language and would come to my room during the period when their classmates were studying regular-level English.

My groups were small: maybe eight at the most and as few as two students. Numbers notwithstanding, memories still abound. For example, the mother of Pedro Rolón, a happy, red-headed first grader, later told me that upon returning home after his first day in Advanced English class, he delightedly told her about the multicolored construction-paper shoes walking along the walls of our tiny space—one with his name on it!

I appreciated the school's subscription to the *Weekly Reader*. Its newspaper-style pages brought us good information from exciting places, encouraged reading in English, and provided activities to act on as desired. For example, the children once created haiku poems after we had read a sampling of them in that little newspaper. The confidence the students gained from their poems was joy-inspiring to see.

Gifts would also sometimes come my way. One of the largest was an unexpected one, brought one Valentine's Day into my classroom by delighted student creators Becky and Mark Esch. The homemade stuffed pillow, in the shape of a bright red heart and covered with silk-textured fabric, probably measured three to four feet long and wide and between one and two deep. It became a delightful piece of furniture for lounging on the floor in our home. I think today, almost fifty years later, we could probably find a snapshot somewhere in our old photo albums of our older son Bryan, just months old, sitting upright, propped up by the cushiony "V" of that valentine.

One day, while I paused in front of the windows between student arrivals, the movement of the clouds caught my attention. I saw them spill over the top of the green-covered mountain slope across the valley and watched them heading directly toward my room. "Clouds in my classroom!" a voice within me sang, "How awesome!" So I waited for the arrival of my foggy visitor. At the precise moment of its entrance—or what I thought to be its entrance—I quickly cranked the metal slats shut. I had caught a cloud in my classroom! A real cloud in my classroom!

Gardening Experiments

In January 1974, our young family of three, consisting of Rafael Falcón, whom I had met and married, Bryan, who had joined our family a few months earlier, and I moved onto the Betania campus. Rafael had earlier accepted the position of school director, following Carol Glick. Our house was the middle one of three near the entry road, with the parsonage on one side and the office building on the other. Since our new home had been vacant for a while, updating it had taken numerous weekends and after-work efforts. But with the volunteer hours of a student's father, our good friend and pastor Enrique Ortiz, and Raúl Rosado, our neighbor in the parsonage, sunlight now streamed through glass windows into our living room area. Fresh paint brightened the walls, and a cozy kitchen welcomed cooking efforts. The transformation took place under the observing eyes of four-year-old Raulito Rosado, who occasionally offered to help.

The move to that house, with its backyard, brought me the exciting possibility of trying gardening, while in the front, two urn-like cement pots invited colorful inhabitants. New to gardening on my own, I wrote to my mom asking her to send me a seed catalog and some seeds from the easy-to-grow crooked-neck squash, which always flourished for us at home. We prepared the ground in the backyard, quite different from the prairie soil of southeast Iowa, I observed, and planted the seeds I had ordered. With Island rains and the suitable temperatures in the Cordillera Central area, results began to show. The sweet corn seeds sprouted! Then, suddenly, weird things started to happen to them. These corn plants grew to about ten inches, developed a top like a tufted weed, and then stopped growing. The squash seeds, meanwhile, never even bothered to show up.

However, my choice for the front pots was more successful. The catalog talked of small orange and yellow flowers that would continue to blossom throughout the season and were ideal for outdoor containers. And indeed, with minimal care, these plants flourished, and I soon had colorful happiness spilling above and over those pots. I was delighted!

Then, one afternoon my husband and I were returning home from a trip. He was driving, and I was absent-mindedly viewing the scenery from the passenger window. I was startled into full awareness just before we accelerated to drive up the steep curving incline of the school entryway. There, abundantly sprinkling the banks of the creek bed under the bridge we had just crossed, I saw myriads of the same yellows and oranges as those in my two urns!

A couple of days later, while in conversation with Don José David, our beloved janitor at Betania, I laughingly related the discovery of having paid for and planted a flower native to Puerto Rican. "*Sí, Missy,*" he gently responded, "I saw those flowers in your pots and considered pulling them out but then thought, well, I guess she must want them there."

Some months later the garden space became unexpectedly productive. A chain-link fence ran behind our home, and the untamed richness of a nature-filled slope lay on the backside. One day I noticed a sturdy green vine coming from that direction, and in the following days, I observed it sneaking through the links directly into our backyard. In a short time, other vines joined it. Gradually they inched their way closer to our house, spreading out over the now-barren area of my gardening attempt. Soon blossoms appeared on the vines, and then—miracle of miracles— little knobs that, without effort, grew into happy-at-home *calabazas*, Puerto Rican–style pumpkins!

New Connections

At about the same time our backyard was going through this freely developing evolution, I left the classroom and moved into a part-time position as a coordinator for the Sponsorship Program. My job was to provide communication between the school and various donors, each sponsoring a student needing help with tuition costs.

To do this, I would send a monthly letter full of chatty news from Betania and would include, at times, an interesting tidbit from the donors themselves. Consisting of individuals, Sunday School classes, small groups, and a business or so, these generous folks often had a personal connection with the school, either having worked on the Island in some role or having participated in a volunteer group at the school. Sometimes, tucked in with the donation check, the senders would reveal interesting happenings in their own lives.

While this was going on at work, one volunteer pumpkin outside in our backyard had grown beyond our expectations. So we picked it, and while savoring its yumminess, we collected a good quantity of seeds. Here the story takes flight. Literal flight.

It all started with idea of sharing the backyard bounty with my correspondence friends. So, in my next letter, I wrote of my gardening adventures and the unexpected gift coming from the back slope. I also included a scattering of the seeds of our *calabaza* in each envelope and sent them through the mail, not knowing for sure what would take place. I did find it great fun to read the responses coming back. One especially evoked a strong "Oh, no!" from me. Along with his donation, this generous gentleman wrote that he had planted the seeds—in his spouse's flowerbed!

Life's Beckoning

During the summer of 1976, our family of three made a significant move. My husband was three credit hours away from earning his master's degree and felt a strong desire to work toward a Ph.D. in Spanish American Literature. The University of Iowa had a good program, and its married student housing could become our new residence. In addition, my parents' home would now be a mere fifty miles away. We were very excited about the university's acceptance and our next adventure!

We also felt sad about leaving but were confident we would return, as it would only take Rafael three years to finish his Ph.D. I can still remember the moment this thinking was placed in doubt. That afternoon, Rafael and I were standing by the sidewalk leading toward the upper-level classrooms, talking with Carol Glick, who would be moving back as director. We would be returning, we said, fully believing that to be true. Carol, on the other hand, expressed doubt.

She was right. In 2011, Rafael retired from 32 years of teaching Spanish American culture and literature at Goshen College. At the same time, due to funding changes, my part-time staff job with the Goshen adult English-learning program ended.

I cherish those five years of my life centered around the Academia Menonita Betania. It holds a special place in my heart. "So why did you leave?" the reader may ask. That's the same question I asked of Romaine Sala, who, with Ray, her husband, planned, built, and then lived for twenty years in the house in Goshen where we live today. "Of all the places we have lived," she told me as we walked around our property some decades after they had left the area, "this is my favorite."

"Why did you move, then?" I asked.

Thoughtfully she responded, "You must go where life calls you."

That has left me thinking. Perhaps like clouds in one's classroom or yellows and oranges on the banks of a creek bed, life's invitations come unsought and unexpected. They just serendipitously show up, it seems, spilling their unexpected challenges and joys into the rich tapestry of the moments of our lives. Then it's up to us, it appears, to give our "Yes!"

Original version in English

26

BETANIA FROM THE 1980S TO THE PRESENT: A PERSONAL ACCOUNT

Antonio Zayas Bermúdez, Ed.D.

Start children off on the way they should go, and even when they are old they will not turn from it. Proverbs 22:6 (NIV)

First Term (1988–1990)

As a child I was blessed to grow up in a home where the fear of God and the study of the Word guided my steps toward Jesus, my Lord and Savior. My mother, Ida Zayas, guided my steps and those of my siblings in the path of the Christian faith. Since infancy, I developed spiritually at Coamo Mennonite Church. My first pastor, whom I remember, was Addona Nissley. Pastor Nissley was one of the conscientious objectors who served in Puerto Rico during the 1940s. I can attest that pastor Nissley's impact on my life helped me discern at an early age the possibility of serving God and our fellow human beings.

I have always indicated that my teaching experiences began many years before I attained my formal teaching credentials. When I was given the opportunity to teach preschool children in Sunday School, I assumed the responsibility wholeheartedly. Since that time, I have not stopped teaching. I grew spiritually as I prepared each Bible class. As years passed, I made a gradual incursion into biblical teaching at higher grades culminating in teaching the Sunday School class for adults. All of this strengthened my faith and helped me listen to the voice of the Master Teacher and hear the plans that he had for me.

In 1984, I obtained my bachelor's degree in elementary education with a concentration in special education. The first educational institution I visited to offer my teaching services was Academia Menonita Betania. At that time, I could not teach at Betania because there were no vacancies. However, by September 1984, I began teaching at Academia Menonita at Summit Hills. I taught fourth-grade classes and classes in the Bible program. In January of 1986, I entered the Department of Public Education, where the Lord allowed me to obtain a scholarship to pursue a master's degree in school administration at the Río Piedras campus of the University of Puerto Rico.

As I was completing my studies in school administration in 1988, the Board of Academia Menonita Betania invited me to consider the position of assistant to the director, who at that time was María H. Ramos de Díaz. The assistant director position became that of full director later that year. This was my first term as director at Betania. At that time, the school offered grades from kindergarten to twelfth grade. This term lasted until the beginning of 1990.

At that time, a sponsorship program offered the opportunity for several students to study at Betania. God had always touched donors' hearts to share their blessings and thus become a vehicle through which students whose families needed economic support could study at Betania.

The 1980s impacted the life of my family in many ways. I started a family with my spouse, Elvia Viera Lebrón, I began my career as a teacher, I received a pastoral call, and I took my first steps as Betania's director. Once I completed my first term at

Betania in 1990, I returned to the Department of Education, where I served as an elementary school teacher until May 1997.

Second Term (1997–2002)

In August of 1997, the Lord called me again to Academia Menonita Betania to serve as the school director. By this time, my entire family was integrated into Mennonite activities. My spouse was secretary for the Council for the Convention of Mennonite Evangelical Churches of Puerto Rico. My children, Lemuel Antonio, Caleb Iván, and Eliezer, were students at Betania. I was a pastor, and I also became the director of Betania. Here I can affirm the words of Jesus from Matthew 11:30, "For my yoke is easy, and my burden is light." Seeing my children grow at the Academia, where the love of God and the life of service were preached in word and deed, gave me the serenity and security that God was guiding our journey. At this time, Academia offered classes from kindergarten to ninth grade.

During this second incumbency, I could see the wonderful way that God worked in support of Betania. We reach many goals during those years. Academic services were expanded when the preschool program began. The Department of School Dining Services of Puerto Rico, now known as the Puerto Rico Food Authority, offered breakfast services. The Academia also tried to open a high school program again by offering tenth grade. This effort was made through an alliance with the Interamerican University of Barranquitas. In this venture, tenth-grade students visited the university campus weekly to participate in language, science, and mathematics workshops.

During these years, enrollment increased year after year until it reached 362 students by the 2002–2003 school year. Private school transportation services helped students from adjacent areas attend Academia. Today, we only have one transportation route that brings students from barrio La Plata of Aibonito, stopping at the Aibonito Mennonite Church parking lot. High gas and vehicle maintenance costs have prevented us from establishing new transportation routes.

An unforgettable event occurred in 1998 when Georges, a Category 3 hurricane, passed through Puerto Rico. The damage to school structures was considerable, with roofless buildings, broken windows, and destroyed furniture. The hurricane hit in all its strength, but the hand of the Lord was with us. Although it was not recognized as an official shelter, people from the immediate community viewed Academia Menonita Betania as a secure location where they could seek temporary shelter after the hurricane had passed and their homes had become uninhabitable. While the government sought placement of these persons in official shelters, Academia Menonita Betania continued providing shelter and aid to the families who sought rest and strength after losing goods and property.

Nehemiah 2:18b reads, "They replied, 'Let us start rebuilding.' So, they began this good work." With this slogan, our work team of Academia launched into rebuilding what wind and water had damaged. Our faith was intact, and we were confident that the Lord's hand would help us reach our goal of starting classes as soon as possible. Before the month was over, Academia was opening its doors to students. Without electricity, without drinking water, but with full hearts, we reinitiated classes. We made many trips to find drinkable water in underground wells. Mennonite churches in Puerto Rico and the United States helped Academia Menonita Betania continue functioning in the aftermath of the hurricane. Staff approached the municipal government for resources to replace roofs, windows, and equipment. For several months, FEMA conducted visits and inspections to ensure the completion of projects.

I will never forget September 11, 2001. On a beautiful sunny day, teachers and students were in their classrooms. María Ortíz, the spouse of the Betania Mennonite Church pastor, Ángel F. Rivera, visited my office. With a sense of urgency, she told me I should accompany her to her house to see what was happening. Her home was on the grounds of the school. I could not believe what I saw on the news. A terrorist attack was unfolding at the World Trade Center in New York City. The phones in the office were ringing continuously. Parents called to pick up their children, given the uncertainty of a possible air attack on Academia Menonita Betania's campus. The next day, the entire staff and students came together for prayer.

By October 2002, I returned to the Department of Education as a teacher, thinking that my contribution to Academia Menonita Betania's history had ended.

Third Term (2018–to present)

In 2017, physicians detected cancer in my body, bringing uncertainty into my life. Eleven months passed from my operation until treatments, radiation therapy, and chemotherapy were administered. As a family, we confronted this situation with hope and faith in the Lord and his power to heal illnesses. During that time, I was director of the Intermediate School for the public schools of Coamo. As I was considering my health situation, I decided to apply for early retirement. By then, I had completed 34 years of service in public and private education. During the entire process, God cared for me. Today I can testify that I was healed in his name. My goal at the end of the process was retirement.

The Word of God says in Isaiah 55:9, "As the heavens are higher than the earth, so are my ways higher than your ways and my thoughts than your thoughts." When I thought I would retire to a life less busy and dedicated to activities other than teaching,

God called me again to collaborate for a third time at Academia Menonita Betania. I retired from the Department of Education on July 31, 2018, and on August 1, 2018, I joined the work team at Academia. Enrollment for that academic year of 2018–2019 was 153 students. Grades served included pre-kindergarten to ninth grade. In my reintegration dialogue at the Academia, I was challenged to add a grade each school year until we graduated that year's ninth-grade class from high school. Last May 27, 2022, we awarded high school diplomas to eight students. Betania again started to graduate students from high school! Three decades had passed since the last high school graduation at Betania. One hundred percent of students who graduated in May 2022 were admitted to the universities they applied to. After several attempts to reinitiate high school at Academia Menonita Betania, we finally met the goal.

Hurricane María in 2017 significantly impacted Academia Menonita Betania's facilities. The roofs of three buildings were blown away. Classrooms flooded. Wind and water destroyed equipment. Many trees fell. Betania was "struck down, but not destroyed," as stated in II Corinthians 4:9b. Once again, teachers, staff, parents, students, and the community came together to restore and rebuild. A great wave of volunteers in and outside Puerto Rico flowed into the campus. With hearts full of hope, the volunteers shared goods and resources supporting Academia Menonita Betania. Step by step, services were re-established and facilities rebuilt in the aftermath of Hurricane María. During the 2018–2019 school year, the Ana K. Massanari building was restored. It reopened during the 2019–2020 school year, thanks to the volunteer labor of sisters and brothers from different Mennonite churches in the United States. FEMA-funded repair projects are still contemplated in the near future.

The Covid-19 pandemic was another event that impacted progress during the 2019–2020 academic year. On March 13, 2020, classroom doors closed. We could not imagine then that they would not reopen until August 2021. Thanks to strong teamwork, the Board of Directors of Academia Menonita Betania, moderated by professor Alex González Labrador, collaborated with the teaching and non-teaching staff to create a plan to continue classes in virtual form. This allowed us to complete the academic year. During the 2020–2021 school year, the skills and digital capacity of parents, students, teachers, and non-teaching staff were tested. Faculty and staff applied methods of distance learning to the teaching enterprise that year. Once again, we can affirm that the hand of God was with us during this virtual learning process, which at first had seemed impossible to attain.

Academia Menonita Betania has fulfilled three-quarters of a century, providing the bread of learning and modeling the virtues of Jesus. Over the years, I have received visits from alumni and former staff with whom God has allowed me to collaborate in this educational work. It is gratifying to observe the sparkle in the eyes of each of them as they relive their experiences at Betania. I listen to their stories mentioning teachers and staff members and talking about specific incidents they experienced as students. I can attest that Betania students forge circles of friends that last a lifetime. I have seen this happening with my children, who are now adults and heads of their families.

I am about to complete 38 years of serving as an educator. God is good. I will be available to God to continue serving in his work, whether at Academia Menonita Betania or wherever he may guide me.

Original version in Spanish

ABOUT THE EDITORS

RAFAEL FALCÓN was born in Aibonito, Puerto Rico. His parents, of Catholic tradition, began attending the La Plata Mennonite Church in 1955 and in that same year registered him as a third grader in Escuela Menonita Betania. After graduating from Betania as a ninth grader and completing high school and college, he returned in 1968 to teach junior-high Spanish and social studies for two years. From 1973 to 1976 he served as the first Puerto Rican director of the school.

Falcón received his bachelor's degree from Inter-American University of Puerto Rico and finished one year of graduate studies at the Universidad de Puerto Rico. He completed his master's and doctoral degrees in Spanish American Literature at the University of Iowa.

He published books and articles on a variety of themes, including Puerto Rican immigration to the United States, Afro-Hispanic influence in literature, Hispanic culture, and Hispanic Mennonite history. In 1985 Herald Press published his *La Iglesia Menonita Hispana en Norte América: 1932-1982*, as well as its translated version. *Salsa: A Taste of Hispanic Culture* came out in 1998, and in 2008 he published a collection of short stories, *Mi Gente: In Search of the Hispanic Soul*. He edited numerous textbooks for the teaching of Spanish as a second language. In addition, together with Tom Lehman, he edited and published the *Colección Menohispana*, ten books on the Mennonite experience in the Spanish-speaking world, focusing on Puerto Rico.

Falcón was a retired professor of Spanish language, Spanish American literature, and Hispanic culture from Goshen College, Goshen, Indiana, where he taught for 32 years.

Rafael and his wife, Christine Yoder, had two sons, Bryan Rafael and Brent Daniel, and two grandchildren, Willow and Sebastian.

Rafael was actively involved in the preparation of this book, reviewing and editing each chapter. His untimely passing on August 17, 2022, deprived him of seeing this book, but his guiding spirit is present throughout it.

TOM LEHMAN was born in eastern Ohio, the son of school teachers who served in mission work for the Mennonite Church in Ethiopia and Puerto Rico. He attended Escuela Menonita Betania for five years.

He completed his undergraduate studies at Goshen College and obtained a graduate degree in Library Science from Indiana University. He retired from the University of Notre Dame Hesburgh Library after working there for 26 years, first as a cataloger and then as Digital Access Librarian.

He edited *My Library Manual* in 2006 and co-edited *Making Library Web Sites Usable* in 2009. In 2013 he published Justus Holsinger's previously unpublished 1970 manuscript *Puerto Rico: Island of Progress*.

Since 2006, he has been digitizing missionary photos taken outside the United States in the mid–20th century. Photos from this collection have been the subject of two books and have appeared in numerous books, magazine articles, and TV shows. They can be seen at www.flickr.com/photos/tlehman/.

Tom is married to Mary Windhorst and has three children, Jason, Kevin, and Jessica. He enjoys paddling and camping in wilderness areas and spending time with his five grandchildren.

Amo a mi Escuela Betania

Mercedes Meléndez, letra

Merle Sommers, música

Amo a mi Es - cue - la Be - ta - nia
Ca - da día en ella a - pren - do
En Be - ta - nia Cris - to es centro
Con la Bí - blia co - mo guí - a

Por su en - se - ñar Por su am - bien - te salu - da - ble
A vi - vir me - jor A - gra - dando a mis a - mi - gos
De nues - tro pen - sar El nos guar - da, guía y sal - va
Po - de - mos ven - cer Po - co a po - co, día por día

Que me ayu - da a cada ins - tan - te
A - gra - dan - do a mis ma - es - tros
En la ten - ta - ción nos ha - bla
Sen - ti - re - mos a - le - grí - a

Lu - chan - do a triun - far
Si a - gra - do al Se - ñor
Gu - ár - da - te del mal
En Je - sús cre - cer

Coro

En Be - ta - nia, Nues - tra es - cuela Cris - to es siem - pre ins - pi - ra - ción

Se - a siem - pre Su pre - sen - cia Nues - tra di - rec - ción

The music for this song is at: https://bit.ly/3ePgnQ2

151

Padre benigno

L.M. Roberts

Desconocido

Pa - dre be - nig - no que en el cielo es - tás,

Gra - cias hoy te da - mos Por el pan que

das. Gra - cias te da - mos, Pa - dre ce - les-

tial, Por el pan del cie - lo,

Pan que es et - er - nal. A - men.

The music for this song is at: https://bit.ly/3xoN11o

APPENDIX B: BETANIA DIRECTORS*
Compiled by Antonio Zayas Bermúdez,
edited by Rolando Santiago

1948–1951: Beulah Litwiller and Clara Springer, the teachers who started the school

1951–1959: Carol Glick's first term; the first official director

1959–1960: Gerald Wilson

1960–1961: John Lehman, substituted for Wilson for a year

1961–1965: Gerald Wilson

1965–1968: Merle Sommers

1968–1974: Carol Glick (Rafael Falcón was Assistant Director in 1973-1974, Falcón & Lehman, 12, in *They Made a Difference,* 2021)

1974–1976: Rafael Falcón, first Puerto Rican director (Falcón & Lehman, 12, in *They Made a Difference,* 2021)

1977–1981: Carol Glick

1981–1982: Jorge Díaz

1982–1983: María H. Rosado de Alvarado, Interim Director along with Carol Click

1983 (August)–1988 (May): María H. Ramos de Díaz

1988 (August)–1990 (February): Antonio Zayas Bermúdez, Coamo Mennonite Church

1990 (February)–1990 (December): Ramón Bermúdez Cancel

1991 (January)–1991 (August): Eileen Rolón

1991 (September)–1993: Scott Jantzi

1993-1997: Lora Miranda

1997 (August)–2002 (September): Antonio Zayas Bermúdez, Coamo Mennonite Church

2002 (October)–2006: Ramón Bermúdez Cancel

2006 (June)–2008 (June): Sheiraliz Bonilla Espada, Coamo Mennonite Church

2008 (August)–2015 (May): Deborah J. Aponte

2015 (August)–2016 (May): Emilio Colón Colón

2016 (August)–2017 (May): María V. Rivera Aponte, Interim Director

2017–2018 (May): Luis Yaviel Vélez Soto

2018 (August)–the present: Antonio Zayas Bermúdez, Cayey Mennonite Church

* No authoritative list of Betania Directors is known to me. Thanks to Antonio Zayas Bermúdez for providing a list that was almost complete. With help from the *Mennonite Yearbook and Directory* and from Eileen Rolón and Lora Miranda the list was completed. However, it is important to note that in a few cases the sources do not all agree on who was director in a particular year. – T.L.

APPENDIX C: PARTIAL LIST OF BETANIA NINTH-GRADE GRADUATES FROM 1956 TO 1980

1956–First graduating class **
    Isaura Delgado
    Rafael Díaz
    Hilda González
    Josefina González
    María Rolón
    Edith Santini
    Grace Snyder
    Karen Troyer
    Luis Vargas
    Unknown
    Unknown
    Unknown
    Unknown
    ** Many thanks to María Rolón and members of the Facebook page *Soy Aiboniteño orgulloso de mis raices* who helped identify members of Betania's first graduating class from the photo shown on the back cover of this book.

1961
    Ruperto Bonilla
    Nereida Blassini
    Minerva Dubbs
    Ramonita Guzmán
    Esteban Núñez
    Elena Ortiz
    Eileen Rolón
    Rafael Soto
    Rafael Vargas

1962

> Ruperto Alvelo
> Benjamin Colón
> Héctor Colón
> Norma Espada
> Ángel Rafael Falcón
> Galen Greaser
> Eugene Hershey
> José Ángel Rolón
> Carmen Ortiz
> Josefina Pavón

1963***

> Andres Díaz
> Miriam Dominic
> Dan Greaser
> David Greaser
> Carmelo Jimenez
> Santiago Martinez
> Fernando Santiago Miller
> Judy Nowman
> Consuelo Ortiz
> Luis Abraham Ortiz
> Naida Ortiz
> Unknown
> Unknown
> Unknown
> Unknown
> Unknown
> *** A member of this class had a graduation photo but
> was unable to identify all the members of the class.

1965

> Luisa Alvarado
> Patricia Álvarez
> Antolín Colón
> Israel Espada
> Annabel Falcón
> María González
> Mark Liechty
> Aurea Núñez
> Elba Núñez
> María J. Ortiz
> Milagros Ortiz
> Aurora Rolón
> David Rolón
> Modesto Rolón
> Raúl Santiago
> Victor Snyder
> Teddy Springer

1966

> Elsie Acosta
> Paul Beachy
> Ricardo Cabrera
> Guillermo Chiesa
> Cindy Driver
> Daniel Espada
> Edwin González
> Josúe Jiménez
> Angélica Méndez
> Edna Méndez
> Esteban Núñez

Domingo Ortiz
Edwin Ortiz
Yvonne Perry
Ruth Rodríguez
Ana Julia Rolón
Migdoel Rolón
Doris Suárez
Wanda Suro

1967

Elsie Acosta
Mabel Alvarado
Enrique Colón
Reynaldo Espada
Joe Greaser
Jim Kaufman
Sadot Méndez
Alberto Núñez
Edgardo Ortiz
José A. Ortiz
Sonia Ortiz
Eduardo Roque
Fernando Rosado
Luís Santiago
Ricardo Santiago

1968

Sonia Alvarado
Becky Álvarez
Lesbia Borges
Edith Borrero
Margarita Colón

Jane Graber
Ángel Feliciano
M. Dolores Hernández
Loida Méndez
Luisa Rivera
Ingrid Suazo

1969

Nathan Baer
Carmen A. Emannuelli
Ángel Espada
Alfredo M. Falcón
John Harvey Hernández
Juan Hernández
José Martínez
Gladys Ortiz
María Ortiz
Hilda Rolón
María Teresa Santiago
Betsy Snyder
Johnny Snyder

1970

Roberto Álvarez
Leonardo Chiesa
Edwin Deliz
Ivette Dhuperoys
Luis González
Ellen Graber
Dennis Heiser
Becky Holsinger
Gladys Hernández

Olga Jiménez
Roberto Miller
Mark Nissley
Glenda Pesant
Marta Román
Federico Rosado
Miriam Soliván
Haydee Suárez
Linda Thompson
Evelyn Velázquez

1971

Lennis Aue
Hernando Avilés
Nivia Cintrón
Samuel Espada
Luis A. González
Rachel Greaser
Lucas Hernández
Lilliam López
Luis G. Martínez
Ruth Miller
Ruth Nissley
Flora Núñez
María Pagán
Orlando Rivera
José I. Torres
María J. Torres

1972

Ricky Álvarez
María Cintrón

Sol Cintrón
Juan Colón
Maritza Díaz
Wilma Espada
Anselmo Fuentes
María González
Robin Helmuth
Daniel Ortiz
Nilsa Pagán
Leida Rivera
Rolando Santiago

1973

Adriano Chiesa
Efrén Colón
Noemí Colón
Samuel Colón
Leonardo González
Víctor González
Ann Graber
Sybil Graber
Roy Helmuth
Eric Miller
Carmen Núñez
Jorge Pagán
Carmen M. Torres
Rubén Torres
María Ramos

1974

Rosita Álvarez
Ángel M. Avilés

Leslie Bonilla
Ronald Boyle
Ada Colón
Eligio Colón
Roberto Colón
Douglas Eby
David Espada
Marcos Falcón
Saribelle Gierbolini
Luisa Hower
John Miller
Wilma Ortiz
Carmen A. Pagán
Roberto Reyes
Ada Rosario
Ismael Rosario
Ricardo Santiago
Ramón Torres
Raphael Vázquez

1975

Elizabeth Alicea
Iván Alonso
Yolanda Avilés
Lucyne Bonilla
Gilberto Cartagena
Jorge Cartagena
Delia Colón
Manuel P. Colón
Rubén Falcón
Alicia Fuentes
María del C. López

Olga I. Hernández
Kathy Miller
Rafael Pagán
Carlos Rodríguez
Francisco Rosario
Lisa Thompson
Raúl Torres

1976

James E. Álvarez
Marta Cortés
Noel Espada
Carmen Gisela Green
Madeline Hernández
Elizabeth López
Bethzaida Ortiz
Olga L. Reyes
Elizabeth Rivera Ortiz
Elizabeth Rivera Torres
Luis Francisco Rodríguez
Vilma Rolón
Erwin Sólivan
Elizabeth Torres
María del Carmen Triana
Carmen Judith Falcón
Ana I. Rosado
Virginia Maldonado
Jorge A. Pérez

1977

Enid Bonilla
Fernando Bonilla

Jaime Vanden Brink
María H. Díaz
Maida González
Eduardo Ortiz
Emerita Rivera
Gerardo Rivera
Sol Magali Rivera
José Ismael Santiago
Jaime Sifre
Roberto Suárez
Nayda Torres

1978

Ivette Arroyo
Jorge Berdecía
Roberto Colón
Ofelia Janer
Hilda Lupiañez
Luis Ortíz
Miguel Rivera
Carmen Rodríguez
Juanita Rolón
Enid Rosado
Walter Valentín

1979

Luis F. Cartagena
Jannette Capó
Rick Nelson Díaz
Marvin Espada
Cynthia Feliciano
Rafael Gil

Sonia Noemí González
Susan Graber
Sammy Hower
Carlos E. López
José Núñez
Maritza Ortíz
Nancy Grace Rolón
Dámaris Rosado
Reinaldo Rosado
Gladys E. Torres

1980

Delis Y. Aguayo
Angel T. Cartagena
Arnaldo L. Cartagena
Jeanette Marie Collaso
Jeanette Colón
Sandra Colón
Melba Espada
José F. Gierbolini
Rafael E. Gierbolini
Steven Graber
Carmen Awilda Hernández
Marilyn Llavona
Luis F. Lupiáñez
José A. Meléndez
Frank Núñez
Modesto Ortiz
Paula I. Pagán
Marcia Kay Powell
Ana L. Rivera
Noemi Rosado

Madelyn Santiago
Roberto Torres
Lizzette Valentín
Zulma Vargas

APPENDIX D: BETANIA PHOTOS

Gerald and Roma Wilson

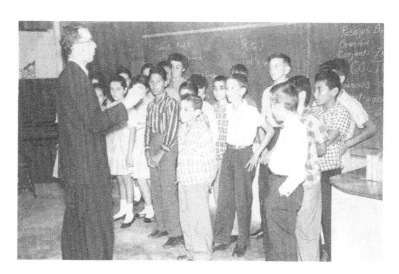

Merle Sommers with music class

Rafael Falcón

Fernando Cains with class

Mercedes Meléndez with class

Carol Glick, Martha Kanagy, Anna K. Massanari, Patricia Brenneman Santiago, Mercedes Meléndez, Doris Snyder

Jerry Heiser and Héctor Vargas

Heriberto Santiago

Dave Holderread

Rose and Rubén Fuentes and family

Anna K. Massanari and Carol Glick

Leroy and Maxine Yoder

Betania staff, 1965

David Helmuth and Ángel Luis Miranda

Betania staff, 1963

Carlos and Mabel Lugo

Patricia and Fidel Santiago

Elmer and Clara Springer

Betania school bus

Betania school truck

Student getting on school truck

Ninth grade graduating class

Betania upper class and administration building

Building with sixth and seventh grade (also science classes)

Elementary class building with windows open

Betania swimming pool

Feeding the school pigs

The Betania dining room kitchen

Lunch tray

Students outside lower classroom building

Betania girls' choir

The Ken Mullet family

Martha Kanagy and Patricia Brenneman Santiago

The Merle Sommers family

Students in library

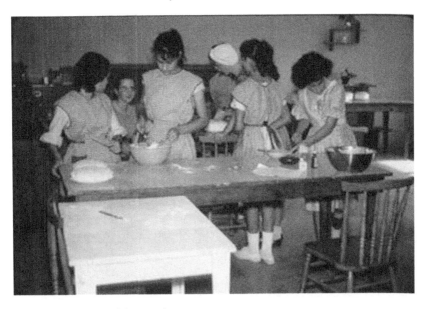

Girls making cakes

Sewing class

Swings and teeter totters

Tetherball

Noel Espada holding black rooster

Made in the USA
Monee, IL
01 June 2023

34823106R10115